Conducting
Made
Easy

for Directors of
Amateur Musical Organizations

by CHARLES J. MEEK

The Scarecrow Press, Inc.
Metuchen, N.J., & London
1988

The author gratefully acknowledges permission from G.
Schirmer, Inc. to reprint measures from "The Lord's Prayer"
by Malotte-Deis on pages 84, 89, and 91.

Library of Congress Cataloging-in-Publication Data

Meek, Charles J.
    Conducting made easy : for directors of amateur musical
organizations / Charles J. Meek.
        p.   cm.
    Includes index.
    ISBN 0-8108-2167-2   ISBN 0-8108-2179-6 (paper)
    1. Conducting.   I. Title.
MT85.M334 1988
781.6'35--dc19   88-18356

In appreciation for the encouragement of my
wonderful wife, Dorothy, a fine musician and conductor in her
own right, who stayed at home to raise our six children while I
spent night after night directing musical organizations for
the extra money needed to feed them all, and for her
expertise in typing and editing this book.

. . . .

Special thanks to my dear daughter, Mrs. Carol Ann O'Connor,
whose fine musicianship and special artistic talent combined to
make all the drawings meaningful.

TABLE OF CONTENTS

PREFACE

This book provides a practical guide for effective directing. It is designed to be helpful particularly to the hundreds of untrained conductors who are directing amateur bands and orchestras, but more especially it can be helpful to choir directors of church, civic, Barbershop and other assorted musical singing organizations.

It is amazing that so many amateur performers do well under the direction of ridiculous hand-wavers who know not what to do or how to do it. But, then, any musical organization may do quite well *in spite of* the director's technique provided there are enough long and tedious rehearsals. In such a case, the amateur performers probably would have done just as well without a director at the final performance. Just think how much more wonderfully they could play or sing if the conductor's directions and signals were always clear, concise, and meaningful.

After more than fifty years of successfully directing bands, orchestras, and church, civic, and Barbershop choruses, and in the same fifty years observing so many examples of crude conducting techniques attempted by otherwise hardworking, sincere, and charming people, I have at last felt compelled to write this small text. May it serve to lend confidence to the aspiring director, improve the technique of those untrained but already trapped in their position as choir director, and, most of all, serve to improve the quality of musical performance.

CHAPTER I

Confessions, The Life of a Conductor

In 1927 my parents took me to a concert in Ohio played by the Lorain County Symphony Orchestra, Eugene Adams conducting. Eugene was a very dynamic director, and in a vigorous passage while making a large sweep, the baton struck his stand and broke in two. The broken end soared to the ceiling of the auditorium, finally landing in my lap. From that moment as an eleven—year old boy, the science and technology of conducting music became an obsession with me.

I had already been studying violin for three years with a marvelous and creative teacher, Yanula Canalos, who later wrote a fine beginning violin method. Little did I know that the following year I would join the Lorain County Symphony as its youngest member. What a thrill it was to play in this fine organization composed of the best musicians in the county, including expert players from the Oberlin Conservatory of Music and with certain specialized parts played by members of the Cleveland Symphony Orchestra brought in for the concerts.

Moving on into high school, I learned to play baritone horn and became student director of the orchestra, the band, and the a cappella choir. I was drum major for two years and directed a dance band. During the Depression, most of the small club dances hired several of the available three- or four-piece ensembles. My dance band was the only "big band" in the county, so we played the big jobs.

During this period, I took voice lessons, and my father often took me to Cleveland for orchestra and opera performances where, I confess, I was more attentive to the style and technique of the conductor than I was to the music.

The family having little money in 1933, I was extremely fortunate to receive a four-year scholarship to attend Oberlin College. I graduated with both a Bachelor of Arts degree, cum laude, and a Bachelor of Music degree with election to the National Honorary Music Fraternity, Pi Kappa Lambda. What a wonderful experience to have studied under so many really great teachers!

I majored in theory of music and composition with minors in violin and music education. Following are brief profiles of some of the teachers and friends who made the greatest impact on my future musical profession:

Karl W. Gehrkens was the nation's most outstanding school music educator, editor of the musical terminology in *Webster's Unabridged Dictionary*, author of textbooks on the philosophy of music, psychology of music, school music, terminology of music, and an outstanding handbook on conducting. When I returned to teach at Oberlin, I was most fortunate to join with him as assistant in the courses on terminology and conducting and to continue instructing the courses upon his retirement.

Victor V. Lytle was an organist, music theorist, and authority on the Schenker theory of analysis. He had a brilliant mind and taught a course on Form and Analysis of musical composition. I studied with him in private lessons to satisfy my honors course in advanced analysis of music.

Maurice Kessler was a former symphony orchestra violinist, violin teacher par excellence, and conductor of the Oberlin Symphony Orchestra, which was one of the outstanding student symphonies in the United States. He was a great director, authoritative but humble, precise and concise in his baton technique, and efficient in rehearsals. He was a master musician.

Arthur L. Williams was director of bands, professor of brass wind instruments, and teacher of introductory and advanced orchestration, at the Oberlin Conservatory of Music. He had an extremely precise and analytical mind and conducted in the same precise and somewhat stiff manner, which was an expression of his personality. He produced excellent results and became the nation's leader in the promotion of new and original concert band literature. On returning to Oberlin to teach, I relieved his heavy schedule by teaching the introductory orchestration classes.

Olaf Christiansen was a wonderful musician who taught choral technique and developed an outstanding a cappella choir in which I had the pleasure of being one of the baritone soloists.

I liked Mr. Christiansen very much even though he taught me, by his conducting technique, what *not* to do. Even so, he produced fine results from the choir, mainly because we rehearsed three times a week with him and knew what he wanted. His wishes were not always evident from his conducting signals.

It was amazing, a little disconcerting, frustrating, and often frightening to an orchestra player to have Mr. Christiansen give a very strong down beat but with no preparatory swing and have nothing happen. One, two, or three beats later, the choir would burst out with a full chord, not always with a consistent waiting period but nevertheless all starting together at precisely the same time. I never knew any member to start too soon or too late. Each of us took a full breath and held it until the spirit moved us. We always felt the start together, and then the director would continue his beat. This worked all right for our a cappella choir members who felt togetherness and could cope with the inconsistencies because of close association with the personality of our director. It was an utter fiasco, however, when occasionally he would be called on to direct a combined choir and orchestra number. The orchestra always came in exactly with his indicated beat. No matter how he explained to us that we should come in as he expected, the orchestra musicians could never master his wishes for a delayed response. He never seemed to have mastered a good preliminary beat. But, however unusual, it worked most of the time for him. It was a wonderfully polished choir.

Normand Lockwood was an unusually sensitive musician who taught counterpoint, fugue, and music composition at the Oberlin Conservatory of Music. He had been a Prix de Rome scholar under Respighi and had been a student of Boulanger. His compositions are well known, graceful, and logical. His ability to inspire his students was exceptional.

Georges Enesco was guest conductor of our student symphony orchestra. A great musician, he seemed to emanate a halo of musical sensitivity surrounding his whole body. His baton technique was clear, precise, concise, electrifying, and inspiring.

Artur Rodzinsky was conductor of the Cleveland Symphony Orchestra. He developed a superb orchestral sound and was a dynamic director. He was always precise, concise, and decisive in every movement. The orchestra always knew exactly what he wanted; every motion was purposeful.

Vladamir Bakalinikoff was a guest conductor at the National Music Camp. He was an imposing figure, authoritative but humble and kind, with a wonderful control of the baton and a superb left-hand technique. One always knew precisely what he wanted. His every musical wish was communicated with perfect clarity.

Percy Grainger was also a guest composer at the National Music Camp. He had a wonderful personality and did much to advance the art of music. Everyone loved him so much that each one always played as if inspired in spite of his conducting idiosyncrasies. The audience had to laugh when he tried to reduce the volume of the cellos in a certain passage. Instead of using his left hand in the customary manner in front of him to indicate less volume, he waved his left hand behind his back on the audience side. The cellos, of course, could not see the hand movement, but the audience could. A great musician is not necessarily an accomplished conductor.

Burrill Phillips was professor of master's courses in advanced orchestration and history of music at the Eastman School of Music. I especially appreciated his deep analysis of the development of musical style, the progress of the development of compositional form and technique, and the unique contribution of each major composer from the music of the early church on through the twentieth-century music. His was the history of musical composition, not the usual history of musicians.

Following college, I became active in the Music Teacher's National Conference, Southern Division, as well as their high school contest adjudicator. I served as director of instrumental music and theory of music in colleges in Georgia and Illinois, which included teaching conducting classes. I organized and directed an excellent group of musicians in Illinois called the Madison County Symphony Orchestra in addition to directing two church choirs, one with an early Sunday service and the other with a late service.

Called back to Oberlin, I taught orchestration, terminology of music, conducting, band instrument classes, and percussion in addition to other duties.

World War II disrupted my teaching career. Because my six children were growing up, I decided to undertake more lucrative employment, so I entered the department of industrial engineering with United States Steel. I had studied math, physics, and chemistry in the process of obtaining my Bachelor of Arts degree. After thirty-three years, I retired, ending my service with the company at the general offices in Pittsburgh, Pennsylvania.

From 1945 to the present, there have been but few months in which I have not directed some musical organization... SPEBSQSA (The Society for the Preservation of Barbershop Quartet Singing in America, Inc.), company choruses, club choirs, community choruses, and church choirs, sometimes as many as four different choirs in a week. Even in retirement I have directed a men's chorus and a Community Concert Band.

Observing and studying the technique of both greater and lesser directors at close quarters for nearly sixty years has been a constant educational opportunity in which I have taken a great and intense interest. I have seen many different methods of attacking such problems as the study and analysis of musical scores, baton technique, cueing, achieving good ensemble and balance between sections, and the handling of the personalities encountered in choirs and instrumental groups. Because of the varying personality, knowledge, preparation, and technique of each individual conductor, results were sometimes good and sometimes very bad.   I have attempted, in this handbook, to analyze and describe the philosophical, psychological, and technical methods that will obtain only the best musical results.

During all these years, it has frustrated me to observe so many honest and sincere directors, who were chosen to direct only because they were good pianists, vocalists, or instrumentalists, but who have not had the slightest idea of proper conducting technique.   Their results have often been sloppy and ineffective. It does not seem to occur to them that it may be their lack of training in conducting that accounts for their poor results.   It simply has been too easy, instead, to blame the performers for their amateurishness when it is usually the director who is at fault.

Conducting is a demanding discipline, equally as worthy of proper training and study as learning to play the piano, organ, or violin, or studying proper voice production. If you wish to be a creative, efficient, and authoritative communicator, you must study well the proper technique of conducting. If you are to be the best possible leader, you must be properly prepared.

This handbook is designed to serve two purposes: 1) To educate the uninstructed *amateur* director in the proper art of conducting, assuming the student to be already a good vocalist or instrumentalist;   and 2)   To instruct all conductors in the art of dealing with special problems of amateur performers.

This book is intended to alleviate the headaches of the hundreds of untrained directors who, because of lack of technical and practical expertise, are struggling with their groups. By really studying and absorbing the lessons in this text, your conducting life will be made much easier, and your results will surprise everyone, even you.

CHAPTER II

The Director's Responsibility

The director may properly be considered the boss but should never consider himself to be the *star performer*. The stars are the producers, that is, the players and singers. The director is only the *catalyst* to a good performance.   Any eccentricity displayed by the director will only distract from the quality of the music and lessen the listener's concentration and enjoyment.

It is sad that a few of our so-called great symphony conductors (as well as choir directors) seem to feel that the audience came only to see them direct instead of coming to enjoy the music.   They often put on a spectacular pyrotechnical display of nonsensical hand and body movements that unfortunately lesser directors sometimes try to emulate.   Remember, however, they are directing professional musicians who would perform just as well, and probably better, without the pyrotechnics. You, on the other hand, are directing amateurs.   Every movement you make must be meaningful if the performers are to understand your intent.   Only in this way can they give you their very best.

The professional director will have previously indicated his desires at rehearsals and is in a position to require his group to obey all the subtleties of his interpretations.   The professional musician must respond accordingly or be fired.   By performance time, the musicians already know what is expected, and they will give the conductor what they <u>know</u> he <u>wants</u> no matter what the conductor does or does not do.

As an example, in the 1930s the Cleveland Symphony Orchestra under Rodzinsky used to do all its encores without the director.   The concertmaster would start them off, sit down, and then these splendid musicians would continue to play exceptionally well, although with a little less enthusiasm and exactness of attack and release.   It was a spectacular gimmick, but it did prove the point that eccentricity is not desirable and that the director can serve as a needed catalyst.

However, you are directing amateurs who try their level best but who often lack strict concentration and attention to detail.   They sing and play strictly for personal enjoyment and the thrill of participation.   You must recognize this difference in purpose and attitude on the part of amateurs.   If your performers make errors, the audience may still consider that the musicians did a great job because they do not expect perfection from amateurs. The performers have little to lose, but you, the director, have all to lose if your directions are erratic or are not clear enough to avoid a sudden crisis or impending catastrophe that can sneak up on you without any warning.

Several qualifications are required if you are to favorably discharge your responsibilities to the performers and to the audience:

1. Learn well and apply proper conducting techniques.
   a. Avoid unnecessary body movements. They serve only to divert and distract the audience's attention and enjoyment of the music.
   b. Control and insist upon clean attacks and releases.
   c. Be aware of balance, nuance, shading, and dynamics.
   d. Command strict attention

2. Personal qualifications.
   a. As a choir director, you must study and know proper breath control, voice quality, and voice projection techniques even though you may not have a beautiful solo voice yourself.
   b. As an instrumental director, you must study and know differences in accoustical tone quality, instrument mechanics, and the technical problems of successfully playing any of them.

3. You must have excellent musicianship to properly interpret the music as the composer and/or arranger intended, including proper tempo, rubato, balance, and phrasing.

4. Reflect in your own facial expressions the mood of the music. The performers will mirror the mood in the quality of the sound they produce.
   a. A smile with happy music.
   b. An unsmiling (but still pleasant) face for serious, moody music.
   c. Never a frown or crabby face.
   d. Never show facial displeasure with amateur performers. It may confuse them and throw them into panic, or worse yet, it may cause them to dislike you altogether.

5. Your expertise in conducting will inspire confidence and enthusiasm in the performers. Remember the following:
   a. Even professional performers make occasional

errors.

b. You can expect amateurs to make mistakes under the extra strain of performance before an audience because they are often trying harder than their ability permits.

c. The performers' enthusiasm will spill over to the audience only if your clear and precise directing has inspired the performers' confidence in you.

CHAPTER III

Mirror perspective

At first glance, you may have thought this chapter would be an article on the use of mirrors to check your technique.   Practicing before a mirror is advantageous and will help you to see yourself as others see you, but the subject is much deeper than that.

In your mind's eye, you must have the capacity to judge your movements according to the particular staging of your choral or instrumental group.   That is, you must consider the needs of the performers standing or sitting in their several positions looking at you in the act of directing. Put yourself in their place, and imagine whether *all* your movements can be made absolutely clear to them. In other words, study yourself in mirror perspective as you imagine the performers looking at you.

Now pretend that you are a violinist sitting in front of a music stand struggling with a difficult passage.   You need reassurance, or maybe you are temporarily lost.   So you look up at the face of the director whose clearness of beat tells you in one *quick glance* that he is on beat two of a four-beat measure.   But what if you couldn't tell it was beat two, or what if you looked up at his face and couldn't see his hand movements out of the corner of your eye at all?

Or what if you were the lead trumpet waiting for an important cue and the director was so vague that you missed it altogether? You watched his face, but out of the corner of your eyes his hand movements were too confusing.

Or, you are a tenor in an a cappella singing group in which everyone is performing from memory. You look the director in the eye, but his gyrations are so unintelligible that your whole section misses the beginning of a beautiful phrase.

In these three examples I have stressed the face and eyes. Yes—the *face* and the *eyes*—for that is where the performers always look. They *never* look directly at the hands. They see hand movement only out of the corner of their eyes while looking at the director's face.

Circle Tilt

If you understand geometry, you will immediately recognize that we can describe an area in which to confine the hands so that the performer can most clearly pick up your signals. That area consists of a circumscribed circle with the tip of your nose as the center and the radius extending to the tip of each shoulder (see Figure 1)

Figure 1

The area defined allows you to direct higher than your head, as when producing the first down beat of a measure. Other beats are produced at or near the shoulder area but never below the heart or middle of the chest. If you extend much below these limits, the performer's perspective of your movements will be lost because he or she *looks at your face.*

The tilt of this circle changes somewhat in relation to your position respective to the position of the performer. It is necessary to keep in constant baton and eye contact. The baton position focuses the performer's observation on your face and has the advantage of projecting the mood in your facial expression.

Imagine that there is a string attached from your nose to the nose of the performer. Obviously, then, if you are on a high pedestal and the performers are all at a lower level, the circumscribed circle will tilt downward so that you should direct lower. The performer's perspective of you will remain the same, however. The reverse will be equally true. Say that the performers are above you on a raised platform. Then you must move your hands higher to maintain the perspective. The guide can always be measured by the respective levels of noses. (see Figure 2)

Figure 2

Side View

We must pursue this a little further before we get to the fundamentals of hand movements. If you put yourself in the performer's perspective as he or she looks at you, you must also consider the performer's position relative to your own. Is the performer directly in front of you, or are you toward the center with some of the performers to each side? You may successfully make many variations in hand movements if all the performers are directly in front of you, but the movements may be quite unintelligible to those performers looking at you from either side.

Let's say that you are directing a large orchestra with the first violins to the extreme left and a little behind you toward the edge of the stage and that the cellos are similarly placed to the right. Or you may be directing a large chorus arranged in a semicircle extending to your far left and right.   Obviously, the perspective of those performers standing or sitting directly in front of you will be quite different from that of those on the sides. You can easily enlarge upon the problems encountered, but here are two examples to get you thinking.

Consider the conducting teacher who has tried to develop a unique style of conducting. He advocates that every beat should travel to a common point as demonstrated by Figure 3.

You can easily determine that his beat structure does not adequately distinquish beat one from beat two or three even to those who are looking on directly. But it is an absolute fiasco if viewed from the side. All the beats look alike, so it is never absolutely clear where the director is in the measure or, indeed, what measure he is in.

Figure 3

Or let's say you have developed a type of one-two beat. For certain purposes, it can be more graceful and "dance-like." This beat may be perfectly adequate if you are directing a very small chorus with all the singers directly in front of you. Such a beat can be illustrated by Figure 4. If you have to look at this beat from the extreme side view, however, the left and right progression of the hand movement loses its perspective and the beat appears to be down, down, down instead of left, right, left.   This is shown in Figure 5.

Figure 4

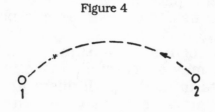

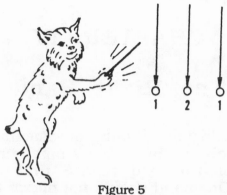

Figure 5

A number of movement idiosyncrasies are practiced by conductors with ill effect, such as "poking" the beat—that is, darting the arm *toward* the viewer in a jerking manner. Obviously, the performer cannot perceive the point of the beat when it is on the same line of vision as his own. Only lateral movements can designate a point recognizable by the performer's eye. Unfortunately, many a stuffy director, full of his own importance, will blame the poor performer instead of studying the reasons for his own inefficiency.

There are occasional legitimate reasons for a variation in beat signals to achieve special effects, but they seldom should be used and then only after considerable forethought. Just as a composer or author cannot achieve greatness unless he or she has first mastered the fundamentals of an art, so also the conductor who has not mastered the fundamentals of directing will be ineffective. Only when he has achieved this mastery can he successfully deviate from time-honored normal patterns.

CHAPTER IV

The Right Hand

The first principle of hand movements in conducting is most commonly unobserved by amateur directors. It seems hard for them to realize that conducting is ambidextrous. One hand should not mirror the other one.

Playing the violin requires the two hands to perform separate functions—the left to stop the strings for pitch control and the right to use the bow for tone control. The player, therefore, must be ambidextrous, for the hands do different things simultaneously. It would be just as silly for a left-handed person to turn the violin around and play it backward as it would be to reverse the piano strings to sound the higher pitches to the left and the bass to the right. *Custom dictates..* It would have made no significant difference had the first instrument been manufactured in reverse and all the later ones had followed suit. There is no "left" or "right" when ambidexterity is required.

There are so many functions and signals to be controlled by the conductor that, to be effective, he also must be ambidextrous. By custom, the right hand controls the tempo, the beat, attack, and release (and upon occasion may be used for cueing if the left hand is busy with other signals.) Thus released from these chores, the left hand can perform other essential instructions such as cueing, control of dynamics, and emphasis.

It is useless for the hands to duplicate each other, signaling the same information simultaneously. First, it is needless and foolish to waste the valuable function of the left hand, and second, it only serves to confuse the eye of the performer who would feel the tempo and the beat much easier if one hand only were used—especially if he has time for only a quick glance during a difficult passage.

Now, let's consider the functional technique of the right hand:

Arm Extension

Conducting movements are produced by a combination of upper arm, elbow, and wrist movements. The upper arm keeps the arm within the confines of the circumscribed circle explained in Chapter 3, "Mirror Perspective," and assists in raising the whole arm up and down to produce the first beat of the measure. Motion is mostly produced by the movement of the elbow. The forearm contributes only a small directional flow in assistance to the elbow movement.

The elbow produces the upward and downward thrust of the first beat and also produces the lateral left and right movements of the arm for all the other beats. Hold the elbow slightly forward of the body in order to place the baton or hand near the facial area, but do not extend the arm too far forward.

The wrist should be flexible but not floppy. It governs the baton movement in delineating the imaginary point that expresses the beat rhythm. The wrist also controls the position and direction of the palm of the hand.

Hold the fingers together, otherwise you confound the perspective with four points instead of one. Most effective, when directing without baton is to extend the first and second fingers, held together. However, never direct with one finger only.

Wrist Action

Stretch your right arm forward with the wrist in a straight-line extension. Now, flex your wrist up and bring it back to the straight line. This may be easier to understand if you place a yardstick under your arm and let it extend past the fingers (see Figure 6) Now, raise the wrist and lower it again to the yardstick. Your wrist should *never* flex below that straight line in designating any beat.

What you will be trying to do is produce a specific point in space that defines the rhythm. The snap of the wrist action will make that point "pop" in such a way as to be recognized and felt by the performer. The pop is produced by the upward flex of the wrist (combined with the direction of the palm of the hand), a movement through the extent of the beat, and then a snap of the wrist (with the wrist in a straight-line position with the lower arm) at the point of the beat as if hitting a nail with a hammer. This, designates the rhythm to the performer.

Figure 6

The Palm of the Hand

In order to produce the snap and pop at the imaginary point that designates the beat, it is necessary that the direction of the palm of your right hand proceed in the direction of that beat.

Hold the palm in a downward position for any down beat. As your wrist rebounds from the snap, turn your palm toward the direction of the next beat. For example, in a four-beat measure, the second beat is to be toward the left. So, on the rebound from beat one, turn the palm toward the left. Proceed through the beat toward your left shoulder, the wrist again flexed, and snap the wrist at the point of beat two. Then on the rebound, turn the wrist so that the palm faces to the right for the next beat, proceeding toward the right shoulder to its point, and so on. The rebound from any snapped beat point results in again flexing the wrist in preparation for popping the next point. Upon trial of this procedure, you will see that you have been forced to make a small loop after each rebound by reason of the turn of the palm. This is entirely proper because you want to convey a feeling of flow from one beat to the next.

Let's try the first beat of a four-quarter measure. Bring your hand high up alongside your ear, wrist flexed. Snap to a point at shoulder level, palm down, using the wrist to pop beat one as explained. Rebound by again flexing the wrist, and immediately turn the palm to the left toward the next beat (or to the right if your next beat is to go that direction as in a three-quarter measure), (Figure 7). You will have automatically produced a beat that the performer cannot misunderstand.

Beat two will travel across the chest at approximately shoulder height, the wrist will pop the point and rebound (thereby delineating beat two), the palm turns right, and you proceed.

The palm, as you can see, should always be turned in the direction of the next beat at the same time as you flex your wrist on the rebound. This permits your wrist to make the necessary snap at the imaginary point. To further clarify this analysis, the palm never is turned upward because no beat is ever produced in an upward direction, only down, left, and/or right.

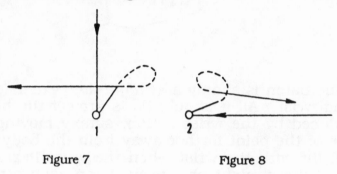

Figure 7   Figure 8

I do not mean by all of this that you should be a contortionist. This technique does not require an extreme 90-degree twist of the wrist to face the palm left or right. Every movement should be natural and relaxed. A slight, or approximately 45-degree turn of the wrist is sufficient.

The Baton

The baton is customarily used when directing a large group because it extends the length of the arm, thereby increasing the accuracy of the perspective, particularly of those performers farther away or in the extreme right or left position relative to the director.

Hold the baton between the thumb and first finger at or near the balance point of the stick. Nestle the ball of the baton loosely in the palm of your hand. If you hold it correctly, it should react in your hand in a manner similar to that of a teeter-totter (see Figure 9).

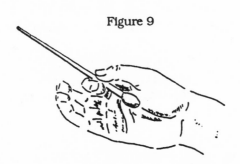

Figure 9

The baton is simply a *straight-line extension* of your arm and wrist. All it should do is project the beat points as produced by the wrist action, simply moving the perspective of the point farther away from the body. The baton will lift with the wrist when the wrist flexes and will return to the straight arm position on each stroke. The *sharp pointed end* of the stick, therefore, is made to designate the point of the beat just as the wrist and fingers do if directing without a baton.

Always

Never

Figure 10

Some directors insist on holding the baton sideways or tipped downward. The image the performer sees in this case is not a single point but, instead, a line a foot long. A line can never project a sense of rhythm; only an imaginary point can do that. Such conductors would convey the feel of the rhythm better without a baton (see Figure 10).

CHAPTER V

The Beat

The most common error I have observed when watching untrained directors is their attempt to direct every note of the music instead of designating only the basic rhythm.. This error comes from a lack of faith that the performers they are directing have the ability to divide any beat of a measure into its component parts.

Almost everyone who has had elementary mathematics in school can recognize that, in 4/4 time, there are sixteen sixteenth notes to a measure. They can quickly recognize that this represents four sixteenth notes to a quarter note and that an eighth note represents a half beat, and so on. If your performers do not know the interpretation of musical script at all, which isn't likely, it takes only a few minutes of explanation to make it clear.

Tempo

It is your responsibility to establish the basic tempo and to designate by your arm movements the primary beats of the rhythm. If you can get your performers to feel the basic pulse of the rhythm, they will divide its components within their minds. If you try to direct all the small details of the note patterns for them, the continuity and flow of the rhythm will be completely lost and the important psychological dependence on group feeling, one with the other, will be destroyed.

You will never successfully be able to define a rythmic beat shorter than half a second. This minimum is the limit of meaningful pulsation that can be felt by the performer as projected by your hand beats. Anything faster than half a second is a mathematical division of the basic pulse that can best be accomplished in the head of the performer. It cannot be meaningfully indicated by the director.

If a composition calls for a speed faster than a basic 4/4—say 4/4 vivace—it is better to direct in a two beat pattern at half a second per stroke (ie., one beat per half note.) It is much more successful to let the performer divide the half note in his or her mind than to attempt four strokes too fast, which will be beyond the performer's emotional ability to absorb. The performer's response is in direct relation to his or her ability to feel the pulsations of the beat. And this ability to experience the musical pulsation is related to a person's physical pulse rate.

Conversely, the maximum speed of stroke that can be felt is approximately one second. If the composition is much slower than this, it may be necessary to designate an intermediary or half-beat stroke (explained later) in order to keep the rhythm flowing. Then the performer will be able to physically feel the musical pulsation.

Geometrical Mechanics

Figures 11 through 16 show the basic movements recognized by custom. They are as important to the director's communication as words are to an author. I will explain some variations later, but all understandable arm and hand movements must be strongly founded upon these fundamentals. Learn them thoroughly, and they will serve you well.

The designs are drawn from the director's view as you would produce them with your own right hand. Figure 11 shows first, the basic direction of the beat and second, illustrates the actual movements of the hand or baton when you combine the arm, wrist , and palm movements. Remember that the wrist flexes at the rebound and will always return to the straight-line position. Never flop the wrist.

It is always important that successive beats be approached from different directions. If the hand moves in the same direction from one beat of the next, the eye of the performer will not be able to distinguish between them.

The directional approach to a beat point is often more important than the exact position of that point. If in the example of a two-beat measure shown in figure 11, the hand approaches beat one in a downward motion, with a rebound straight up, and if the two beat is also down, a quick glance will not show the performer whether you are on the first or second beat

Figure 11

Basic Direction	Actual Movement	Time Signature
		2/2, 2/4 or fast 4/4 or 6/8

This problem is solved in the two-beat pattern by rebounding the arm to the right after popping beat one, thus forming a loop beyond the position of your beat two. This permits you to approach beat two in a left-hand direction instead of another downward motion. The mechanics are as follows: From a point near your ear, with your palm down and your wrist flexed, stroke to point one. Rebound to the right but not higher than half the length of beat one. Because the rebound will have carried you to the right beyond the position of beat two, you must turn the palm somewhat to the left to pop beat two. Rebound upward to the starting point while turning the palm down. This automatically produces a curved or bellied line. Now you are prepared for the next down beat.

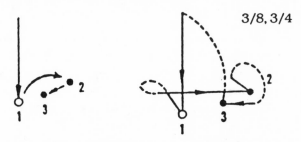

3/8, 3/4

Figure 12

All first strokes to beat one are the same. In Figure 12, showing the three-beat pattern, turn your palm to the right at the rebound. This automatically produces a left-twist loop. Direct your arm and flexed wrist to the right edge of the circumscribed circle in order to pop beat two. Flex your wrist on the rebound, turning your palm to the left, thereby making a right-twist loop. Direct your arm and flexed wrist to the left, near where point one was in order to pop point three. Allow your arm to rebound upward while turning your palm down. This produces a little belly in the upward line because of the turn of the wrist.

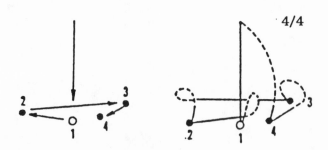

4/4

figure 13

Figure 13 illustrates a beat for 4/4 time that is like the immediately preceding one except that beat two is to the left. Consequently, the rebound from beat one produces a right-twist loop because the wrist turns the palm to the left as the arm travels to the pop point at beat two.

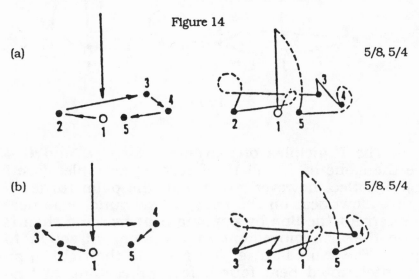

Figure 14

(a)

5/8, 5/4

(b)

5/8, 5/4

Consider the movements shown in Figure 14(a). In this example, beat two is the same as the 4/4 beat in Figure 12. Notice, however, that beats three and four travel in the same direction. The point at beat three interrupts the line with a snap and rebound. With the palm still turned toward the right, the arm proceeds to beat four. You will also observe that the two diagrams in Figure 14 delineate two- and three-part divisions within the same measure. Study the composition's beat pattern to decide which to use. Most commonly, the composer does not significantly vary the pattern throughout the composition. The pattern may be 12-345 in which case use the beat formations in the upper diagram. If the composition clustering were 123-45, you would use the lower diagram.

I need not show a seven-beat illustration because it is so unusual that you will probably never run across such a composition. However, the principle is the same as the 5/8 pattern in Figure 14 (a) except there are more interruptions in both the left and right lines. Most seven-beat patterns are 123-4567 or 1234-567.

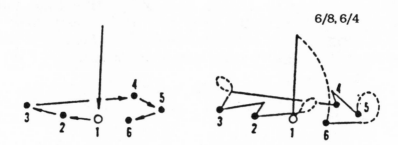

Figure 15

The Principles of movement for 6/8 and 6/4 time are the same as for all the foregoing examples (see Figure 15). Notice, however, that with the palm turned left after the downbeat on the beat one rebound, it is necessary to interrupt the line by popping beat two and then to continue the arm movement in the same direction to beat three. The same is true for going to the right to produce the interrupted beat four before proceeding to beat five. Make sure that beats three and five are within the confines of the circumscribed circle (Figure 1) if you want the performer to see and feel the pulse of the beat.

Larger Denominations

You probably know that the time signatures are indicators of measure and always show the number of notes of a certain value in each measure of the composition. A 4/4 time signature means that there are four quarter notes in each measure. In 6/8 time, eighth notes are the basic composition symbols, and there are six of them in each measure. It is a matter of simple mathematics that can be conveyed quickly to the rankest amateur.

Larger denominations of measure, such as 9/8 or 12/8, can be directed simply enough by using the patterns of smaller denomination that have already been described. The nine-beat measure is 3 x 3/8. Therefore, the use of the basic three-beat movement is adequate. Your arm simply remains still at each major point in the three-beat pattern while two extra wrist flexes snap two extra beats, as shown in Figure 16.

Figure 16

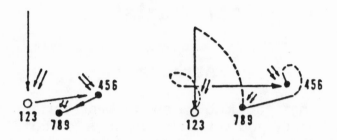

Just as in the three-beat measure, the direction of the palm remains the same as the primary beat for each extra tap. That is, the arm is holding still for each cluster of three pops of the wrist. In this case, the palm turns right after the rebound from beat three and left after the rebound from beat six. With palm turned to the left, the wrist pops the beat seven count, and the arm stays there while the wrist strokes beats eight and nine. The palm does not turn down preparatory to the upstroke to produce the next beat one until after the beat nine rebound.

In this kind of compound beat pattern, the arm and elbow are used to place the hand and wrist in position for the first beat of the cluster. The second and third beat of the cluster are produced entirely by the wrist movement, snapping the rhythmic beats at or near the point of the first beat of the cluster.

Similarly, a 12/8 denomination is really a 3/8 measure multiplied by four and can be directed as just explained but with a basic four-count beat per measure.

Notice that these cluster beats should be used only if the tempo is slow enough to warrant a pulse on each eighth note (approximately a half second each). If the tempo is much faster, then ignore the triple clusters and direct the simple three- or four-beat pattern. Let the performers feel their own triplets.

CHAPTER VI

Beat Variation

At the Gate

Now that you know how to beat various types of measure, how do you get the performers to start?   How do you get them to attack the first note precisely together?

There are those directors with such limited faith that they feel compelled to give a whole measure of beats before the starting measure to be sure the performers will respond properly.   Others with a little more faith may give two beats ahead of the starting note.   This is unnecessary and inadvisable and probably leads to more confusion than it tends to help.

One preliminary beat ahead of the starting note, if you execute it properly, is sufficient.   You can easily train the performers to follow your direction explicitly so that they will attack exactly together.   The principles involved are as follows:

1. Prepare your tempo in your mind first.

2. Raise your hand to let the performers know you are ready.

3. Wait for their full attention before starting.

4. Just before the starting note, make one preliminary stroke exemplifying the beat.
   a. Make the starting stroke for this preliminary beat somewhat shorter than normal.
   b. Make no snap of your wrist at the preliminary beat point because you don't want the performers to start there by giving them any kind of positive indication.   Just move through the stroke smoothly.
   c. Make sure the preliminary beat is in exactly the same tempo that you plan for the start of the composition.
   d. Turn your wrist and palm just as if you had snapped the preceding point, thus giving the rebound movement the illusion of a beat so that the performers can feel the upcoming tempo.
   e. Produce a much larger loop than normal as you proceed toward the starting note point.

5. Snap your wrist to make a positive beat at the point where you want the performers to start. Do not pussy-foot here; be decisive.

6. Remember that you negate the snap if your wrist flops below the straight-arm position.

If you are directing a chorus of singers, not only does the preliminary beat set the tempo, but it tells them when to take their breath preparatory to the entry attack so that they can all come in together. Almost all the performers will come in with you immediately, but it is not uncommon at rehearsals of a new composition for there to be a few stragglers. Start over several times if necessary. Quite often, the stragglers will shame *themselves* into coming in with the majority. If this happens, you will have few problems starting any other number afterward.

If one or two tenors, on the other hand, consistently come in ahead or behind the others, then first practice the start with only the tenor section. If they do not correct the problem immediately, you will notice that the rest of the organization will be looking at the culprits. There will be no need for *you* to embarrass them by picking on them alone unless it becomes absolutely necessary. They will usually see the point before you get frustrated. In case they have so little awareness that they do not catch on, then you may have to pick each one out individually—or tell them to wait until intermission and you will work with them on it. In any case you must realize that they are interested in doing a good job or they would not be there. You know they are doing their best. So use good humor instead of criticism to let them know that you want to help them. They will need encouragement at this point.

Starting Beat One

Let's assume that you are starting in 3/4 time and that you want your group to start on the first beat of the measure. Put your hand in position and say to yourself in tempo "one, two." Now, as if *after* the rebound from beat two (see Figure 17), start your hand in a short preliminary beat in the direction of beat three, with your palm left. Pass smoothly in tempo through beat three point without any snap, but turn your palm down as you normally would do. Make a larger belly than normal on the upstroke. Proceed to near your ear, then down positively to pop beat one where the performers are to start. If your preliminary beat is consistent with the tempo you will be using, the performers will sense the start perfectly (providing you do performers will sense the start perfectly (providing you do not use a floppy wrist).

Figure 17

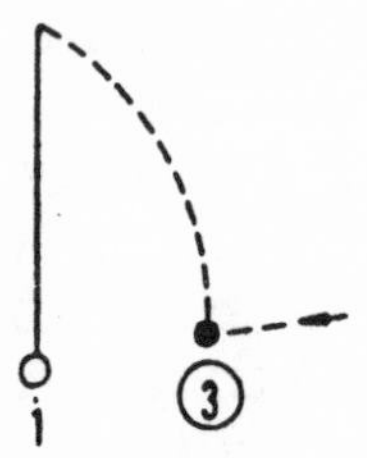

Starting Beat Two

The general principle is the same if you are starting on beat two: a short preliminary downbeat to one but with no snap. Proceed smoothly in normal fashion but with a larger loop, making sure that your preliminary beat reflects the exact tempo. Then pop the starting beat two very positively. Remember that your palm turns exactly the same as in producing a normal beat pattern.

Figure 18

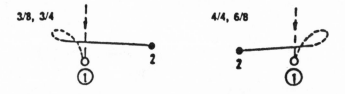

Starting Beat Three

To start on beat three, move from the position of the prior beat (whether left or right) but always with a graceful larger loop in tempo. The larger loop makes it possible to be more positive in giving the starting beat

Figure 19

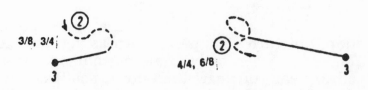

Starting an Offbeat

You will have no problem in starting your group on any offbeat if you indicate a strong and decisive primary beat structure. The right-hand movements are precisely the same as in starting beats one, two, or three as applicable. Make a preliminary stroke, and snap the primary beat just before the offbeat.

Your responsibility is to provide a strong rhythmic pulse. The performers will provide their own feel for the subdivision of the beat. If you attempt to indicate the subdivisions for the players or singers, their inherent feeling for the primary pulse will be interrupted and destroyed. If you should feel compelled to try to direct a sixteenth note in 4/4 time, you lack faith in your group's ability.

Let's consider a couple of examples;

Figure 20

The composition shown in part in Figure 20 starts on the "and" of beat three, which is followed by four "and" one. Hold your right hand, palm left, at the position for beat two. Start by turning your palm to the right to form the rebound movement of beat two, flow through the preliminary beat, and pop three. Now, make a sharp rebound off beat three with an enlarged loop. If your pulse is positive, the performers will have no trouble feeling the half-beat.

The example given in Figure 21 requires that the performer feel the quadruplet subdivision of beat three. If your preliminary beat is forceful and designates the proper tempo, and if you pop beat three vigorously, then the performers will enter confidently. They will easily produce the three sixteenth tones and come in exactly with you on beat one.

Hold your hand at rest, palm right, as if you were ready to pop beat two. To start, flex your wrist and turn your palm to the left to produce a fair-sized loop. Bring your arm to position for beat three, pop the point vigorously, and proceed to beat one.

Permissible subtleties are sometimes very effective. Because the first note in measure one is a half note, and providing all parts hold for the two counts, you can minimize your stroke on beat two in preparation for a stronger beat three in measure one.   This will tend to force a crisper response on the quadruplets.

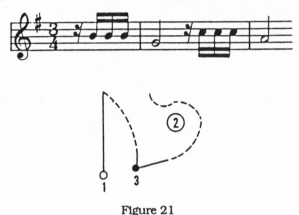

Figure 21

OFF AND RUNNING

Once your group has started, there is another consideration regarding tempo. If the speed of the composition is slow, it is best if you extend your beat to the limit of the circumscribed circle (Figure 1) because you need to express spaciousness and continuity and to give the impression of an easy gracefulness.

As the tempo quickens, make the extent of your beat pattern smaller, in reverse proportion. The reduction in the spacing of your beat, left and right, should bear a direct relation to the speed of the tempo. This aids in the visual perception of your intent and will be felt by the performers. The size of the beat is a communication tool.

Similarly, if you want to retard any single beat a little, widen or elongate the space when proceeding toward that beat. Your hand movements can be very expressive. Should you wish to produce a rubato effect, shorten the beat strokes when picking up speed and lengthen the strokes on the retarded ones.

Should you come to a fermata or "hold", make a wider and more positive right-hand movement to cue the performers that something different is about to happen. Then simply come to a stop, no matter what the beat. If the piece goes on, after the hold, continue with exactly the same arm and wrist movement as if there had been no hold, or use the cutoff movement if applicable.

Another tool in your comunication kit is the style of your beat. You can express joy or sadness; your beat can dance or shuffle; it can be quick and stiff or expansive and graceful; it can convey solidity or liquidity. All these are done by your control of the type of stroke, whether it be a quick movement with the beat points sharp and precise, or smooth with the beat points precise but not angular.

You may occasionally need one more type of beat variation—the rather angular half-beat movement. Certain compositions by their character (or certain measures within a composition) seem to emphasize a half pulse. Many directors identify this beat by saying "1 and 2 and" where the feeling for the "and" is strong. You may want to express this, particularly if the tempo retards much or if the composition calls for a tempo in which the primary beat structure exceeds a beat per second.

The half-beat pattern consists of sharpening the otherwise free-flowing loops at the rebound points of each beat. The palm directions remain the same, but the arm and wrist produce a more angular rebound at each rebound peak, producing a secondary point. This point is marked by a momentary stop action, as illustrated in Figure 22. When you try this, you will notice that it is mainly the wrist-flex snap at the rebound that produces the secondary half beat. The rebound from the last beat of the measure, however, is taken all the way to the peak of the down stroke on beat one. This half-beat pattern is best used only if the music is sharply delineated and vigorous. If the character of the music is smooth and free-flowing, you can express the flow of the music better if you would simply use a double tap as if it were a two-part cluster (as explained in Chapter 5).

Figure 22

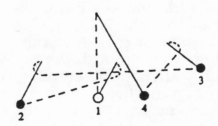

THE WINNER

In most activities, the one who reaches the goal first is the winner and the last is the loser. Not so in music. If one performer comes in too soon or if another is left hanging on when all the others have stopped, everyone in the performance loses.

Clean attacks are most important but no more so than clean and precise releases. Listening for good attacks and releases is the quickest way to identify a well-rehearsed group and an excellent director. If your conducting technique puts you in the category of an expert, everyone is the winner.

Let us consider how you stop the performers once they have run the race to the finish. Some conductors simply lower their hands until they are out of sight. This will result in each performer's independent judgment as to when to stop. It will surely be a ragged ending if the performers cannot see what the conductor's intent is. Many movements will accomplish a release of tone, whether at the end of a phrase or the end of the composition. In all cases, you must make a positive and decisive indication if the movement is to be recognized.

If the music ends sharply on a designated beat in a forte passage, simply make the hand movement exaggerated and very positive. If the ending is in a soft passage, you need not make the movement so vigorous and perhaps not so exaggerated.

If it is appropriate to hold the last beat, whether to effect a crescendo or diminuendo before the cutoff, or simply to hold at the same intensity, it is usually sufficient to arrive at the beat in the normal manner, use stop action as in a regular hold, and then twist the wrist quickly with a snap for the cutoff.

The left hand is often useful as an assist in designating a release, but it is not often necessary to use it because the action of your right hand can clearly and sufficiently indicate your intent. For instance, let us assume you have come to the last count on any particular beat. If you want the performers to hold the last tone and at the same time to effect a crescendo, then slowly raise your baton hand. As long as it is moving upward, the performer will know to get louder until you snap the cutoff. (Your left hand may also be signaling in a different way for a crescendo which will reinforce the perspective.) This movement is diagrammed in Figure 23. If you want a held diminuendo, the reverse is true. Your hand will gradually descend until the point of cutoff. In this case, make sure your arm movement to the last beat is carried higher than ordinarily so that you have room to lower the arm and still permit the release snap to be within the limits of the circumscribed circle so that the performers can see what you are doing. These are the simple but positive methods to assure that your performers do as you desire. These methods will work even with a group you may be directing for the first time.

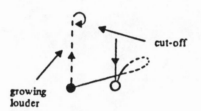

Figure 23

There are other ways, however, that are quite effective if the performers know before hand what to expect. For example, there is nothing wrong with a bit of showmanship when directing such organizations as barbershop choruses. If your chorus knows you are going to do it, they will hold the last tone while you turn around, a big smile on your face, both arms extended as if inviting tremendous applause, then snap the arms down for the release. Be sure, no matter what method you use to effect a release, that your movement is decisive, and that your deportment is appropriate to the occasion.

Before we proceed to the next chapter, it is necessary to make one further comment. If you are directing a mass chorus with orchestral or band accompaniment (or with soloist), it is necessary to continue to direct the instrumentalists when there is an independent phrase or passage in which the singers are at rest, because there are so many musicians requiring direction to keep them together. Don't forget to cue the chorus back in when their turn comes around again.

Conversely, let's say you are directing a church choir or a glee club with piano or organ accompaniment. It is absolutely *unnecessary* for you to direct one individual when the singers are at rest. The pianist or organist is probably the only trained musician in the group besides yourself. Why insult that person's musical ability by pretending to direct a wholly instrumental passage? The organist probably will ignore you in any case and play the passage his or her way, which is that person's right as I view it.

Your responsibility is to the chorus. Simply cue them in at the proper time when the organist arrives at the chorus entrance. There is one possible exception. You may be expected to set the original tempo at the very beginning of the composition. Once the organist has started with your tempo, it is time for you to quit until the first chorus cue.

CHAPTER VII

The Left Hand

Unfortunately, most trained or undertrained directors do not recognize their insufficiency. They tend to think that they are doing all right even though the performers do not give them all they are demanding. It is easy to blame the performers instead of ourselves. It is hard to admit to ourselves that we really do not know what to do or how to do it. Just try to explain to a director how he might improve his conducting technique and see how intensely he resists and ignores your willingness to help. He may need aid badly, but he has great difficulty recognizing his inadequacy—and in his own mind he probably sees no reason to improve.

Such a director is one who constantly uses his left hand merely to mirror the movements of the right hand. The performer, from the viewing side, becomes somewhat confused seeing two hands going in opposite directions simultaneously. It is as if the director expects the performer to move the left eye in one direction and the right eye in the other at the same time. Besides the inherent confusion, it is a shame to waste a valuable communication resource.

Left-hand movement can be a most expressive tool in communicating your intentions to your performers. It is your instructional guide to musical interpretation. It should *never* be used simply to duplicate the movement of your right hand. If you momentarily have no interpretive instructions to display, it is best to drop your left arm or hold your left hand steady at your waist in a position of complete inactivity. Constant needless flailing about of the left-hand or duplication of the right hand's movements can result in a monotony that breeds inattentiveness similar to that caused by a cymbal coming in on every beat of a band number. Use the left hand only when you have something important to say with it. Otherwise, let the right hand do all the speaking.

Nevertheless, the proper use of the left hand is of paramount importance and, together with your facial expressions, is an essential tool in the technique of conducting. The following sections explain some of its uses.

Holding the Left Hand

The eyes can perceive a single unit more readily than a multipronged unit. Therefore, hold the fingers together most of the time so that the hand presents a single unit. There are occasions, such as cueing, when the two fingers nearest the thumb may be used for greater specificity, but it is inadvisable to use a single extended finger, which looks awkward and is harder to see by the performer.

Furthermore, if you use the single finger approach, there is greater tendency to "poke" at the performer, which is one of the most ineffective movements you can make.

Cueing with the Left Hand

Combine left hand cueing with eye contact. Before the entry beat for the individual performer or section (such as the baritone soloist or horn section), look them directly in the eye or at least in their direction, so that they will know you are about to cue them in. The preliminary movement of the left hand usually occurs one beat before the cue. If special attention is required, however, you may raise your hand into the preparatory position several beats ahead to alert the particular player or section.

Now, hold your left hand at rest as if in readiness, at a point well within the circumscribed circle until your right hand has reached the position representing the preliminary beat before the cue.   When your right hand reaches the rebound point of this representative preliminary beat, raise your left hand in much the same manner as used in the preparatory movement of the right hand at beat one, using a flexed left wrist, no matter what beat the right hand is indicating. Simultaneously and in conjunction with the right hand exactly at the point of entry, let the left hand move down and snap the point.

If you have established eye contact, then you need not make the movement of the left hand large—just plainly visible and precise. You will notice that only on beat one will one hand be a mirror movement of the other. In all other cue beats, the left hand proceeding up and down will be at variance with the left-right movement of the right hand. It may take some practice to be able comfortably to move the two hands independently.

A right-hand baton cue is sometimes advisable if the left hand is already busy with an important signal. It is also sometimes easier if a performer is at the extreme right side of the conductor, which makes it unnecessary to turn your back to the left side. In this case, leave the circle area and make the movement toward the player very positive, and make eye contact. If both hands are occupied, it is effective to cue by using the necessary eye contact with the individual or section and simply nod your head at the moment of entry.

Loud - Soft

The palm of the hand is used as a communication tool in everyday life. In traffic control, the palm forward universally means "stop"; the back of the hand with waving wrist means "come on"; a vigorous waving arm movement means "come here quickly."

In music, the left hand is equally expressive. It is universally recognized that the palm turned upward means "grow louder" or "give me a crescendo." The palm turned downward means "grow softer" or "diminuendo."

You can intensify the crescendo by moving the whole arm slowly upward (with palm up). You can attain maximum fortissimo by ending with your fist closed and your arm held high. Appropriate facial expressions may further intensify the performers' efforts.

You can signal the diminuendo with your palm toward the viewer and further intensify it by first raising your arm, then turning your palm downward while lowering the arm until the performers arrive at the dynamic level you are seeking. If they don't respond as fully as you like, then, while lowering your arm, you can allow your hand to approach your lips as if to tell them to "shush."

As you can see, the left-hand movements are totally independent of the right. Variations of these basic movements will occur to you as you feel the need for them and as the musical effects demand them.

Control the Unruly

What if the top tenor section, or the percussion, or any other section is so loud it overbalances the other sections? The same left-hand movements described earlier for loud and soft are applicable. But, in this case, look directly at the offending section, possibly sweeping your eyes over the group to let them know you are including all of them, and give them as much of the "shush" technique as required to soften them down.

If a section is too soft and underbalances the rest of the group, encourage them to give you more by any variety of the "come-here-quickly" technique. Again, the general sweep of your eyes, not fastening them on any individual, is the cue that you mean to include the whole section.

You may use the same technique even if it is a single individual who is overbalancing a section or if you want more of the person's expertise to shine through the music. Whatever the reason, it is necessary for you to make individual eye contact with that person, holding your eyes on that performer so that the rest of the section knows you don't mean them, and signal clearly to the person your immediate advice in this particular situation.

The Release

There are a few occasions, such as at the final fortissimo ending of a composition, when you may want to be doubly forceful on the final cutoff by using the left hand to reinforce the action of the right hand. Bring the left hand into play only on the preliminary of the last beat, possibly with fist closed, and bring the fist vigorously down simultaneously with the right hand in a kind of hammer-thrust.

The left hand mainly is more commonly used as a tool to effect the release of a phrase affecting one section while the others continue to play. That is, the right hand continues to direct the rest of the group while the left hand cuts off the section. You can most easily effect the release by a quick twist of the left wrist, having already put the hand in place somewhat ahead of the release to call attention to the impending action—all, of course, accompanied by eye-to-eye contact.

The same action may be required to effect a clean cut-off involving an individual who has just completed a solo phrase, such as an oboe in an orchestra composition, especially if the soloist's last tone has been held for several beats. Here, again, individual eye-to-eye contact is essential.

Quality Control

The left hand can be useful in a variety of other ways as well. It can intensify any signal appropriate to the right hand, such as accents *on* or *off* the beat. It can hold one section while others continue as, for instance, when tenors hold for four beats while the other singers change harmony on each beat. Or it can indicate a cue on any portion of an offbeat while the right hand continues to stroke the main pulse.

An almost endless variety of signals and combinations of signals is possible. One of these, related more directly to singers, is a signal to encourage better quality of tone production. For instance, in rehearsal you may find the basses forgetful or reluctant to produce a round, pear-shaped "Oh". At some subsequent performance, you can assure the quality of production by making eye-to-eye contact with the bass section, forming an "O" with the fingers of your left hand, placing the left hand near your mouth, and producing a big fat "Oh" with your lips.

The left hand can assist in solving any anticipated problem. The methods are numerous. Just make sure you have studied your method from the standpoint of the performer who will be watching the action of your hand. If you try some method and it does not work well, think about these fundamentals and devise a method that does work. Never blame the performers. If they cannot understand your signals, it is your fault.

Sharing

Can you wink and produce a very large smile? If so, you should do well in encouraging your group, particularly if you genuinely feel they have performed exceptionally well. Or, at least, as well as you know they are capable of doing. After all, they are amateurs.

Figure 24

At this point you may reinforce the wink and smile with the traditional "OK" sign held up near your eye (Figure 24). It will please the group to know you approve of their efforts. You can expect your encouragement to carry over in enthusiasm to do even better.

Last, do not consistently take all the applause yourself. Graciously share the accolades with your group at each performance (but not necessarily after each number). Step gracefully aside, your arm extended to the singers. Or, if the musicians are seated as in an orchestra, have them rise. Then, stand aside and give them the accolade. If you do this, your group will love you all the more.

CHAPTER VIII
No—Noes

Decorum

Mr. All M. Portunt
Figure 25

A wonderful friend and true gentleman liked to direct civic amateur choruses. He was a well-trained musician and able conductor, but he wanted everybody to know it. He always brought four batons to rehearsal. Then, in front of the chorus, he would take each out of its case, weigh it carefully in his hand, and select the one that best suited him that particular night. (Pretty professional, ??) Having made his selection, he would start off the rehearsal talking about "the diminished chord following the augmented ninth in the fourteenth measure" and then follow that with something like "the second number for rehearsal tonight, as you know, is in the phrygian mode." The rare disease known as "arrogantium pomposis" finally did him in. If you were to do similar overbearing things to your singers, what do you think they would say behind your back?

The director must be a critic of all the elements of good performance. She must be capable of remedial surgery for any problem as it arises. She should make corrections in a good-humored way. She should never make any remark or insinuation that could embarrass a performer. Helpful criticism is beneficial. Derogatory criticism is detrimental.

Madam Krit E. Sizer
Figure 26

Maybe you can't feel bouncy and enthusiastic all the time, but a good showman will never reveal it to his group. If you don't look forward with enthusiasm to the prospect of a rehearsal or performance, then perhaps you should look for another profession. If you are perpetually a crab and your frown reveals your cantankerousness, your group will be uncooperative and will lack enthusiasm to produce to their capacity. Even your best friend may not tell you that you suffer from extreme "facial-expression-halitosis."

Mr. Crab N. Fraun
Figure 27

Distractions

Mr. Tow Tapper
Figure 28

While your upper torso is busily involved in expressing the rhythm, why is it necessary to tap a toe that no one can see except the audience? Such distractions, no matter how gracefully done, tend to cause the audience to concentrate on the distraction. Wouldn't you rather have them listen to the music?

Mr. Heal Rocker
Figure 29

If you raise your heel, even in proper tempo, your knee is forced to bend, jogging your whole body. Do you think that this will prove to the audience that you really feel the rhythm? More probably your group will suffer due to the resulting shaky beat pattern. More assuredly, the audience will be little impressed by the music.

Mr. Futz Tomper
Figure 30

Maybe the audience would enjoy seeing your foot stomp, particularly if you do it rhythmically. Some very ineffective directors do such things. Why not you? But you can be sure your performers will not appreciate it.

As you try to designate the point of the beat, the bouncing knee simultaneously moves the point to another position. It could be very confusing to the performers. Can you imagine what they might say behind your back?

Ms. Nee Baunse
Figure 31

Mr. Bott M. Wiggler
Figure 32

Wiggling your bottom may bring a certain amount of joy or satisfaction to some members of the audience, but you can be sure these listeners will remember little of the musical performance.

Mr. Shold R. Tosser
Figure 33

If you constantly move your shoulder as you produce each stroke, your beat will be floppy and indecisive. Maybe you will decide that this is your unique method of conducting so your group had better get used to it. After all, you are the professional. They're only amateurs.

Mr. Hedd Wagger
Figure 34

You may suppose that wagging your head from side to side and occasionally up and down will be a great attention getter and you will be right. Who cares if it interferes with your eye-to-eye contact and tends to confuse the precision of your beat. But would you want your audience to say, behind your back, that even though you moved your head most gracefully, they can't remember much about the musical performance?

Technique

Mr. Am B. Guity
Figure 35

Mr. Am B. Guity is a director whose biggest claim to fame is an inconsistent beat encompassed by an incomprehensible pattern. How wonderfully free your group will feel not to be restricted to conformity. I'll bet their attacks and releases will blow the mind of the audience.

What would you do if you heard your best tenor say to another behind your back, "Wish I were cockeyed. Then my left eye could follow his right and my right eye his left hand. I'm having trouble taking in the contrary movements."

Mr. Dubb L. Hanbeet
Figure 36

Mrs. Avery Nota Beeter
Figure 37

Suppose you overheard your favorite soprano say to her husband, "Can't feel the fundamental pulse when this gal is directing. Wish she'd let *me* feel the sixteenth note instead of her interrupting the flow of the beat. And she never does it the same twice."

Mr. Otto Site
Figure 38

Can't you imagine your group saying to themselves, "I know that handsome devil is on the podium, but I can't see what he's doing."

Wouldn't your most faithful performer say, "Hey, Mr. Director, what's your point?"

Mr. Flop E. Rist
Figure 39

Mr. Beib I. Waver
Figure 40

If you should copy a director who does this, can't you envision your entire group thinking that, as long as you insist on waving goodbye, why don't you just leave right now. In such a case, I believe they could do just as well without you.

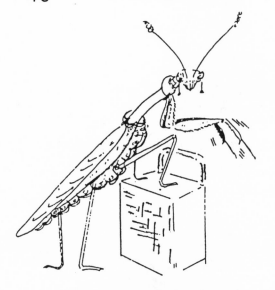

Miss Stif N. Ockword
Figure 41

What if you produce no preliminary beat, no wrist snap, no fluidity, no expressiveness, no nothing! Suppose you make every movement square, rigid, and stiff. Then you're probably dead. No one would be able to feel your pulse at all.

P.S. The probability of producing a "No—No" is greatly reduced if you keep your feet close together. Good directing should be accomplished from the waist up, with no overt movement from the waist down, and with feet comfortably close. Always stand well balanced and relaxed. This is pleasing to an audience and, as well, will help you to define and project a better and more efficient beat.

CHAPTER IX

Problem Traps

Facial Expression

Facial expression is an important function of conducting. You have only your hands and your head with which to show mood. The movement of your hands, the type of beat, the size of your gestures, the varying speed of movement from one point to another...all these assist in delineating the tone, nature, and meaning of a composition. The head, lips, and especially the eyes are effective complements of these gestures. Your facial expression intensifies your hand signals and helps to clarify your every intent.

The eyes are one of your most important tools. Eyes can be magnetic. A quick, sharp glance can be a warning; a soft, open-eyed glance can reflect satisfaction and confidence. A squint can scold, admonish, and reprimand.

The eyes are extremely useful when cueing a soloist or a section, but it is necessary to establish eye contact before the cue. Always be assertive in coupling your downbeats and accents with constant eye contact, especially when making the initial beat at the beginning of a composition or on new phrases. Extremely ineffective conducting will result if you bury your eyes in the score. You will have lost an important and eloquent resource for communication.

If you naturally have a poker face, you will do much better becoming a gambler than seeking a vocation or avocation as a conductor. Professor Karl Gehrkens, who wrote a successful book on conducting in the early 1920s, always put on a radiant smile when he started to direct. He taught us much by example, and it did have a major effect on us. His smile boosted our confidence, increased our joy in singing, and made us all the more assured of his authority.

A half smile can signal pleasantness; a broad smile can signal satisfaction, approval, and an anticipated joy of living. Relaxed lips may indicate self-confidence, tenderness, or poise; firm and rigid lips may indicate resolve, decisiveness, or determination. If your mouth is turned down at the corners, it can mean sadness, meanness, or disapproval.

Even the tilt of your head may send signals. Holding your head slightly lower may signify attention, intensity, or deliberation, but if you hold it even lower while looking upward with your eyes, the effect could be intimidating. By dropping your head too low, however, you run the risk of losing contact with your performers. Sometimes lifting your head slightly might signal pride, pomposity, formality, or strictness. Nodding, with eye contact, is often effective in cueing. With all these subtleties available, it is not necessary to roll, rock, or shake your head, movements that are often distracting to both the audience and the performers. Neither are these movements a clear or understandable method of communication. A frown, on the other hand, may throw amateurs into confusion for they most often will not understand the reason for so severe a sign of disapproval.

Both the audience and the players can instantly recognize insincerity, pompousness, and aloofness, and they will react negatively. Always be understanding and pleasant with your performers. In particular, be pleasant and graciously appreciative of a good audience reaction. A big smile and graciousness will pay big dividends.

Remember, your performers, either singing or playing by memory or looking up from their music stands, will always look at your face. They will see your hand movements out of the corner of their eye. It is important to direct in the circumscribed circle (Figure 1) so they can both easily take in all the subtleties of your baton and hand movements as well as monitor the changes in the mood of the music as those changes are reflected in your face. If you can make your gestures and your expression completely complementary, your performance will be exciting and inspirational.

You can easily be trapped into overexpression, aloofness, pompousness, or even the reverse, a lack of expression. Do only that which is germane, appropriate, and relevant to the faithful expression of the music.

Cueing

I have already covered the technique and methods of effective cueing, including the use of the left hand, the baton, and the nodding of the head, all in conjunction with eye contact. There are a few traps into which the over-enthusiastic director may fall, however, so I wish to reemphasize a few points.

No movement of your head, baton, or left hand should ever be overmagnified. In making a cue movement, your left hand should be crisp, to the point, and completely supportive of the right hand. Never prolong the cueing gesture beyond its immediate usefulness. Over-using it can be a direct insult to the intelligence of the performers.

It is better to hold your left hand at your waist with the hand closed easily (if opened flat against the stomach it may look as if you need an antacid) or near your heart so that it will be ready for instant action if needed. If you were to hold your hand completely at your side, the cueing would require a large, obtrusive, and distracting move-ment.

Generally, you should not draw audience attention away from the enjoyment of the music, and certainly bad cueing technique will do this. But if it is done unobtru-sively, it may sometimes help to guide the audience to recognize some of the interesting countermelodies and/or the special activity of solo parts within the superstructure of the composition.

Remember not to point with one finger when cueing. The chances are that you will fall into the trap of jabbing at the player which, because it is in his direct line of sight, he will not recognize accurately. Either keep all fingers tightly together, or extend the index and second finger held together using an up-down movement for the cue.

Many conductors use maximum cueing at the begin-ning of rehearsals on a new number. At the rehearsal just before the performance, they often will use only a few cues or even none at all. They feel that this causes the per-formers to be more attentive during the concert. There is some truth to the thought that you can wear out the effect of cueing and that, by reducing their use at the last re-hearsal, the conductor's cues will have greater impact during the concert and will give greater control of prob-lems as they arise.

But beware! This procedure can confuse and alarm amateurs, who prefer that you always be consistent. It makes them comfortable and secure. However, even with amateurs, be stingy in the use of cues. Use them only when absolutely necessary.

The trap is the tendency to overconduct your cueing. As with a garbage can, you notice it the first time you smell it, but as you become accustomed to it, your nerves shut off and you pay it no more attention. If you overconduct, the minds of your performers shut off.

Fermatas

Fermatas are often very troublesome to most musicians, in particular to directors who have to decide exactly what the composer intended, how long to hold the fermata, and what technique to apply in order both to interpret it properly and to induce the group to execute it properly.

The fermata is a halt, delay, or pause in music and is indicated by the symbol ⌒. *Fermata* in English means a temporary stop or rest indicating that the tone should be prolonged. But how long should it be held? This question is solved by studying the character of the music, the basic tempo of the composition, the dynamic requirement, and the underlying flow of the phrase.

The term and its symbol have been used for more than four centuries so that its meaning and use have slightly changed over that period of time. One of the problems of interpretation is to decide whether the composer intended the fermata to mean a hold longer than that of the indicated value, or a hold of the full value, or whether it is a direction not to perform the tone staccato. The fermata has sometimes been confused with the direction called *tenuto*, which is often abbreviated "ten." Tenuto really means to hold to the note's true, full value. With some composers, particularly those of several centuries ago, the fermata may be simply a mark of a cadence point not meant to be held at all.

It is therefore impossible to assume a strict value relationship when the fermata is used. Some musicians erroneously maintain that the fermata always means to hold twice, or even three times, the normal value of the note. There are, however, rather rare cases in which a composer will have tried to indicate more specifically what is meant by writing such indications "poco" meaning little, or G.P. (gross pause) meaning a great pause. In most cases, it is left up to the director to use his own judgment.

Two questions must be decided. First, does the fermata require a cutoff release, or is it on an active chord requiring a resolution. If the former, the fermata is simply a delay that overflows into the next chord or phrase. If the latter, it requires no cutoff at all. You pause in your beat, and the release is automatically accomplished by the normal rebound in preparation for the next beat. Examples of this are found in Chapter 14 "Applied Techniques."

You must also consider the location of the tone in the phrase that contains the fermata. If it is indicated at the end of a phrase and has the necessary feeling of finality, you should probably give it a cutoff release. If it is in the middle of a phrase that seems to require subsequent motion, a feeling of progressive overflow, you need not give it a stop cutoff movement. All agree, however, that the fermata should not destroy the feeling of musical flow unless a special effect is called for.

The trap for the conductor is to recognize which type of fermata he should be directing and then to arrange the cutoff or the overflow release in such a way that his hand is in a position that is adequate for continuing the beat pattern without any lost motion.

The Music Stand

One of the problems least recognized by directors is the arrangment of his physical surroundings. Can every one of the performers see him clearly? Can he see them? Are they arranged so that they can hear one another? If the performers are in an orchestra or band, are their stands positioned so that a quick glance will put the director's face in full view?

Most of these problems are obvious and evident. Often, however, the conductor will neglect to consider the arrangement of his own equipment, which can have an important or even drastic effect on his ability to communicate directly with his players. What he does with his paraphernalia is in direct relation to his position in respect to the group. If the group is below where he stands, he must direct lower to maintain the line of sight. If the group is higher, he must direct higher. The placement of his music stand will also be affected. Now suppose that the conductor is to stand on a podium that is on a level with the performers. If he is directing a choir from memory, he has little further problem with equipment. The score of a chorus is relatively simple, and although it usually takes the same amount of technical conducting skill, the parts are few and therefore easier to control.

The conductor enters in a businesslike manner, dignified and poised. If the audience gives a grateful amount of applause, he will turn toward them, smile broadly, perhaps nod, then turn around and step on the podium or, if there is no podium, step into position.

An orchestra score with its multitude of parts and sections, or a band score, which can be even more complicated, usually requires the conductor to use a music stand upon which rests the score. As conductor, you should know the score perfectly, but its complexity demands that you be able to refer to it quickly in case of memory lapse or some other crisis. There is a host of countermelodies and individual instrument entries that also requires that you have the score before you.

Your first duty is to check the music stand and be sure you have the correct score. If necessary, adjust the stand to approximately waist height or a little lower. It should be relatively flat, tilting slightly toward you. Now test its position with your left elbow extended horizontally. Can you turn the pages without interfering with your conducting gestures: Can you easily read the music? Can you do both in an unobtrusive manner and with no wasted motion? Is your position completely compatible with the beat area and eye contact?

Having satisfied these questions, stand back six to eight inches to make sure you can adequately view the music without dropping your head to read it. A constant movement of the head up and down can be very distracting to both the players and the audience.

Take a natural, comfortable stance, standing squarely on both feet. If your arrangement should make it necessary for you to squat, your posterior can be very unattractive to an audience, or if you would find it necessary to bend your knees, it will surely disrupt your beat. Take note of the chapter on "No-Noes."

Stand with your feet nearly together or slightly apart to gain a comfortable balance, perhaps placing your left foot slightly forward to gain equilibrium with the operation of the right hand. The music stand is a locale of quick focus that pinpoints your face and your gestures.

Remember to give your musicians time to adjust their stands so that they can see you easily with a quick glance from their music and feel perfectly acclimated to your location. If you are directing a choir that is singing a cappella, make doubly sure they have taken the proper pitches before you begin. When all is ready, raise your baton, carefully make the proper preliminary rebound stroke, and deliver the starting beat positively.

Remember, if you have only one person accompanying who has an introductory passage, just start the accompanist off, then wait until time for the group entry before you direct further.

Stand relatively still when directing. Make conducting movements from above the waist. Too much body movement disrupts the musician's line of sight. It also draws audience attention to the director, which disrupts their concentration on the musical performance. Excessive movement as well as overconducting ceases to be meaningful. Use your beat technique to avoid turning your back on any section of musicians. Your profile is a distraction to the audience, and the musicians behind you will not be able to see your beat or read your intentions.

CHAPTER X

General Tricks

Committees

As the director, you are the catalyst for the successful operation of any musical group. You should be the leader in all matters concerning musicianship, rehearsal methods, and technical application. The organization may have committees set up for different purposes such as arrangements, staging, membership, publicity, and the like.

The music committee, however, should always include you as a member, even if ex officio. You should be invited to all their meetings. It is sometimes hard for amateur musicians to realize that they may not have enough practical knowledge of technical detail to make a reasonable or responsible decision in some cases. They may not realize that final judgment on music matters must be left to an expert. They tend to feel that, because they have sung or played music for twenty years or more, they have the equivalent of a Conservatory of Music education. You must insist upon the right to overrule the committee in case of necessity.

Such cases of necessity may often arise. Usually they involve decisions concerning musical quality, as in the following examples.

1. The committee is enamored with a particular number. To them, one arrangement is the same as another, so they pick out an arrangement made for professionals in which the range for sopranos reaches high C. None of your singers can successfully sing beyond G. Your committee might not recognize the problem and invest in fifty copies. There is no way you could successfully teach them such a song.

2. The committee, not recognizing that variety is the spice of any program, selects five slow, sweet numbers for the next concert.

3. The stage committee insists the chorus would look better if it were standing in a straight line.

Curtains and drops absorb vibrations, and sound is lost to the auditorium area. As a consequence, the sound does not return to the singers well enough for them to hear each other. You, on the other hand, want the chorus in a semicircle so they can hear one another as they sing.

Confidence

It is your responsibility as director to do everything possible to inspire the confidence of the group in your ability and, in turn, to inspire the group's confidence in its own ability to perform well. Your job is to be an interpreter and to pass on that interpretation to the group in clear and concise hand movements. This can be accomplished only by knowing your music thoroughly. Study the phrasing, the dynamics, the entries of each instrument or section, the holds, special attacks and releases, the words, and so on. Above all, you must be constantly aware of each individual's actions and reactions by strict observance and accurate listening. Train your ear to hear each individual singer or player, identify any problems, and be ready for any required solution.

Study the composition to determine the composer's and/or arranger's intent. Be faithful to the proper tempo and phrasing. You are the *interpreter* only; you are not the composer.

Take the Pitch

In an instrumental group, it is customary for the concertmaster or any other designate to silence the group and call for the pitch. For orchestra, the pitch will be A because the strings are in the majority. All stringed instruments have an A string from which they tune the other strings.

In a band, the pitch is more often a B-flat, which falls naturally in most instrument's harmonic series. The instrument usually selected to give the pitch is the oboe because it has the greatest difficulty in adjusting its double reed mouthpiece to vary the basic pitch of the instrument.

Once the pitch is given and held long enough to be accurately heard and remembered, the concertmaster will indicate either a section-by-section tuning in the case of rank amateurs or, more commonly, will allow mass tuning to take effect. When satisfied that all are in tune, he again calls for silence, the audience quiets down, and the conductor enters, we hope to tremendous applause.

A chorus, on the other hand, having probably undergone a previous warmup in another section of the building, moves into position on stage followed directly by the conductor. Quite often there is no applause because this procedure is less spectacular. But no matter. Here the whole situation is quite different.

If the chorus is accompanied by a keyboard instrument, there will be no problem with establishing pitches. But if the chorus is to sing a cappella, taking the pitch properly is all-important. Given improperly, it leads to confusion. You may then find the tenors starting off in the key of G while the baritones and basses begin their singing in the key of F. I have heard these major fiascos on a number of occasions. The problem is easily remedied. No matter what the entry chord is, whether the tonic, dominant seventh, or other, it is best to sound the pitchpipe tone only on the tonic. That is, if the composition is in the key of G, then blow a G. If the key is E-flat, then blow an E-flat. Figure 42 is an example of what I mean.

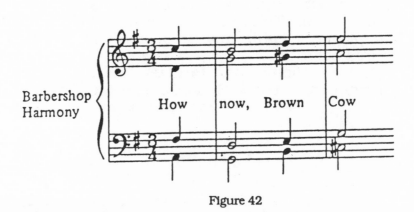

Figure 42

The tonic (or I chord) is on the primary beat of the first measure preceded by an upbeat chord on the dominant seventh (V_7). You should blow the G for the tonic first. Let the chorus hum their tonic chord until you are sure their consciousness has absorbed the tonic perfectly. If they have trouble selecting their pitches, have them all hum the tonic G first, then the top tenors and baritones move to *mi* on B. The top tenors hold, and the baritones proceed to *sol* on D. This sounds out the first primary tonic chord, which establishes the tonality of the piece. Then, by a slight hand movement, you may indicate for the chorus to back up from the tonic pitches to the starting chord on the dominant seventh.

If you do not do this, but instead blow the D as the root of the introductory seventh chord, the singers will not have had the opportunity to absorb the tonic in their minds. They may hit some foreign chord on the word "now." Certainly you run the risk of their singing the whole song out of tune. A feeling for the tonic in any composition is an essential.

What if the chorus has trouble taking their pitches from a pitch pipe? The remedy is to practice some vocal exercises on *do-mi-sol-do* , first in unison, then by "break apart." That is, basses hold the *do* , the baritones hold *mi* , the lead tenors go to *sol* , and the top tenors proceed to the high *do.* It should take no imagination to apply the same principle with a mixed chorus. In such a vocal exercise, have them sing the actual solfege words, *do-mi-sol-do.* The words will assist by supplying a meaningful symbol to attach to the musical notation and will provide auditory recognition.

Although having perfect pitch is not necessarily an advantage over good relative pitch, it is sometimes useful if you have several in the group who possess this attribute. While you are turned around receiving applause and/or making remarks to the audience, the "perfect pitchers" can hum the tonic, the chorus can take their pitches quietly, and when you turn around may move backward to the introductory chord, such as the dominant seventh as in Figure 42. If all is done quietly enough, the audience will be unaware of the action. When you start directing, the chorus will have appeared to have started "cold" without any pitch taking at all. It can be rather spectacular.

Listening to One Another

It is important to train your group to listen to every other section, be your performers an instrumental group or, more especially, a singing group.

I remember attending a regional Barbershop Contest years ago. One of the quartets was without question highly trained. It was said that each of the four singers had absolute or perfect pitch. The tenor blew the pitchpipe a short blast, but they did not sound out the tonic chord to check their intonation before starting, so confident were they. Each obviously knew his individual part perfectly. He could sing his own part solo from beginning to end and stay on pitch. How wonderfully they might have sounded had they taken the trouble to establish the tonic in their minds before starting. Also, they should have hummed the starting chord, to see that it rang clean and clear. The end result was that each sang their individual part as if singing solo oblivious of the others, all in a different key. Not a single consonant chord was distinguishable. Each paying attention to his own perfection only, they seemed not to be aware of the other's presence or tonality. It was the strangest musical performance I have ever heard in my long musical career.

There is little danger of this happening to your group, but if the tonic is not fixed in the minds of your singers, they may sing through to the end of the composition with each of the sections struggling constantly to adjust the intonation, one with the other, without success.

Even if you are successful in impressing the tonic in their minds, there can be other troubles. With amateur singers, it is not uncommon for an individual in a section to sing out of tune with his or her other colleagues even when the first pitch is taken correctly. This often is the result of an untrained ear or, more probably, to bad voice placement. You are not there for the purpose of giving private voice instruction, but it is best that you work with this section only, for a small time, in order to remedy the matter.

Have the section take its pitch. Have all of its members listen for an extra long time to the tone in order to seat the pitch well in their tonal imagery. Use "ay-ee-ah-oh-oo" vowels slowly, either one at a time or in combination, on a single pitch. Hold the tone and make the section's members listen to one another. It is interesting to hear the individual voices adjust. When they blend as one voice, you will know they are listening properly.

Even more important, each member of a particular section must develop the ability to hear every other section. Orchestra and band musicians are more likely to have developed this ability because they have spent so much time studying music and wrestling with the difficulties of their instruments. And they have had much more opportunity to play in a variety of groups. Their struggles have made them more capable of awareness of others, whereas amateur singers have not had to endure such strenuous effort.

There are several ways you can help your performers develop awareness of their colleagues:

1. It is always necessary to position your singers so that it will be physically possible for them to listen to one another. If at all possible, arrange them in a kind of semicircle. The ones in the center can more easily hear the sections on each side. The ones at the extreme edges will be singing in one another's direction and can also

easily hear those in the center. If you are in concert, the audience will hear them as well as if they were in a straight line but, oh, what a difference to your chorus members!

2. At rehearsals, you can select any short chordal passage. Forget the words, concentrate on vowels only. Sing each chord on various vowels very slowly, not moving to the next chord until each is sufficiently tuned. If any particular chord is not right, do not move from it until it **is** right. Use your left hand to indicate to a section the necessary adjustments up or down to bring them into tune with the others. They will be pleased when you get each chord to "ring." A chord absolutely in tune is bell-like. The choir will know when they hit it, and the smiles on their faces will be your special reward.

3. The most out-of-tune choruses are likely to be glee clubs or church choirs who sing only with accompaniment. Most often, the director will have spent no time teaching the singers to listen to one another. It is characteristic for them to listen only to the piano or organ to sustain their pitches. But pianos and organs are temper-tuned, each tone being an approximation of the true natural harmonic series. This is necessary because a keyboard instrument must be able to pass from one key to the next at random. Its construction does not allow a player to adjust the pitch.

Most other instruments are capable of some tonal adjustments...the strings, the trombone, and the voice infinitely more than others. A chord, to ring properly, must reflect the natural harmonic series that is based on purely mathematical relationships of the overtones of the fundamental of the chord. In order to ring, the third, fifth, seventh, or ninth of chord must be related exactly to the fundamental overtones. Any acoustician can easily demonstrate this principle.

The remedy is to require your chorus to sing a cappella at least part of the time. Use the procedures given in paragraph 2. There are always phrases and passages, even in accompanied music, that can be isolated for a cappella practice. Make your performers listen to one another. Better yet, choose a few numbers specifically written for a cappella singing to add to your repertoire for variety. The benefits in the improvement of your group's singing will be tremendous.

4. This item concerns deep breathing. No one can take a really deep breath if his or her chest cavity is restricted by poor posture. Encourage your group to sit comfortably and relaxed, but they should be erect with legs uncrossed. A singer or wind instrument player should not lean against the back of the chair because it will restrict the expansion of the rib cage. If the singer is standing, he or she should poise naturally and comfortably, erect and relaxed, with weight on both legs evenly.

5. If the chorus uses music, have the singers hold the music high enough so that the smallest movement of their eyes from the page will put you in view. Do not allow them to bury their noses in the pages.

Discipline your group as soon as you take over as director. Let them know immediately that you know the techniques that will be most helpful in developing a fine musical group. The little things are often more important than large ones in striving for success. Do not let your performers get away with anything that may be deleterious to the total effort. But always keep your good humor.

CHAPTER XI

Technical Tricks

Rehearsal Time

The quickest way to discourage your performers is to waste time at rehearsals. More can be accomplished in one hour of concentrated, well-planned, and skillfully controlled practice than any two-hour, relaxed, slow-moving, uncoordinated, and unplanned rehearsal.

Years ago I was invited to become the new choir director for the largest church in a small town. The previous director had held two-hour rehearsals starting at 8:00 p.m. on each Friday evening. The choir consisted of four men and twelve women, all wonderful people but not sufficient in numbers and with the parts too unbalanced for a successful singing group.

Analysis of the problem indicated that the most interesting events of the week, in both school and community, occurred on Fridays. I also knew that a one-hour rehearsal that was well planned with no wasted time would be adequate. It was agreed to hold rehearsals starting at 7:00 p.m., quitting exactly at 8:00. There was much skepticism at first. Soon, the choir found out that rehearsals in no way interfered with other community activities. Young people could now sing in the choir and still enjoy a date on Friday evening. Within a few weeks, the choir expanded to a stable 30 members, all the choir loft would hold.

If you are to develop a successful, harmonious, and happy group, consider these points:

1. Select a day convenient to the majority.

2. Select a time of rehearsal that least interferes with other community activities.

3. Keep rehearsals short and snappy.

4. Waste no time, save your jokes, and minimize talking and explanations.

5. If one section tires or shows strain, let them rest while you use the time constructively working with other sections.

6. If rehearsal time is packed with efficiency and of short duration, there will be no need for recess.

7. Follow your commitment exactly. Let the performers go on time.

Consonants

Proper pronunciation and enunciation of words in singing require vocalization on principle vowels only. Consonants may be considered as attacks and releases surrounding a vowel. Consonants should be clearly enunciated but only as a kind of rhythmic "brake." About the only problem you will have with consonants is to make each singer synchronize at the same instant. An expert cutoff hand movement will most often solve this problem.

The hard "s" sounds, however, sometimes are troublesome and in several ways. The problems result from words ending in "ce," as in "since" or "x," as in "six," or when one word ends with "s" followed by another starting on "s," as in "Let's sing." Occasionally an "s" carried over into the next word will give surprising results. Note the following, for example:

1. Are they singing "this tory" or "this story"?

2. Are they singing "six sheep" or "sick sheep"?

3. In a song about "the Cross I'd bear," would your choir sing instead about "the crosseyed bear"?

Be alert. Your singers will want to produce the right sound. Any chorus will gain the most enjoyment if its members are confident they are singing correctly.

There may be a tendency to close the vowel off too soon and sing through the consonant, particularly if the word ends on a "liquid" consonant such as "l," "m," "n," or "r." This can be controlled by proper explanation, practice on different words, or holding the tone longer with sharp cutoff.

One other common problem is what I call the "pollution effect." Even if your cutoff is snappy, some performers are faster in their reactions than others. Particurlarly if the word ends on "s," you may hear a flood of "s" sounds that will congest the acoustical atmosphere. The "s-s-s-s" may sound from all directions, which may make your chorus sound very unprofessional. If you cannot find a suitable method to remedy this, you might suggest that they close off with a soft "z" sound instead. The combined effect will sound like an "s" anyway, and the sharp multiple "s" sounds will melt into one.

Vowels

Many words employ single pure vowels. Most of our vocal problems, though, commonly occur on compound vowels or dipthongs. The primary or entry vowel is the one to be held and vocalized. The secondary vowel comes off at the very end of the tone in the same manner as a consonant would to finish the word. Consider the following example:

Word	Primary Vowel	Secondary Vowel
how	hah	oo
soil	soh	ill
nice	nah	ees
night	nah	eet
pout	pah	ute
time	tah	eem
day	da	ee
quite	kwah	eet

The problem is compounded for the untrained singer if these types of words are sung on two or more tones and, sometimes, even on a single tone if it is held for several beats. The untrained singer tends to sing the primary vowel on the first tone and change to the secondary vowel on the second tied pitch.

Figure 43 shows a typical example of the technique of the amateur versus the professional.

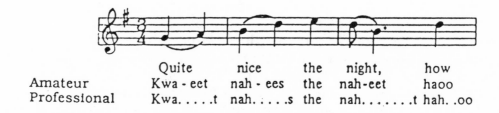

	Quite	nice	the	night,	how
Amateur	Kwa - eet	nah - ees	the	nah-eet	haoo
Professional	Kwa.....t	nah.....s	the	nah......t	hah..oo

Figure 45

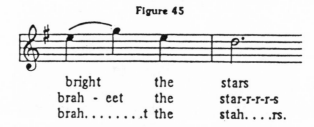

	bright	the	stars
	brah - eet	the	star-r-r-r-s
	brah.......t	the	stah....rs.

Figure 43

Precision

Depending on how well the group responds, it may be necessary to devise special exercises to gain precise response. Precise attacks and releases are necessities for a good performance. Be consistent in your interpretations in the final rehearsals before a concert. Often much can be gained by varying tempos, interpretations, timing of attacks, and extended holds before release in a practice session. It can become a good-humored game to teach your performers to concentrate and to watch you closely. It is not necessary to do anything wild...something just mildly unexpected will do. Every now and then you may catch a culprit napping, one who came in too soon or held on too long. Treat it as a game to achieve strict attention to detail for the good of all. Never use the exercise to embarrass the individual...only a positive indication for the performer to shape up.

You must know all the words if the group is to sing a cappella. Individuals or sections may have a temporary lapse of memory that could cause a phrase to collapse. If the chorus is not too sure of itself, you may be able to avert a fiasco by mouthing the words just ahead of the singers. It is even helpful just to mouth the first word of each phrase because the first word is often the critical point.

Hard Swipes

Hard swipes is Barbershop harmony terminology, but it can be meaningfully applied to the music of any singing group. The dictionary indicates that a *swipe* is a strong blow delivered in a sweeping motion. Indeed, a musical swipe is a strong group of chord changes that sweep across any held tone to "juice up" the arrangement. If done badly, it is no better than a stale beer.

If a swipe or other passage is especially difficult harmonically, it sometimes can be "washed out" by singing the passage backward, then forward again. If you try this, drop the words, use a single easy vowel, and move slowly from one chord to the next both forward and backward. It will quite often save time otherwise devoted to individual part rehearsal and tedious fitting of the parts together.

Swipes expertly written can be learned quite readily. If they are difficult, it may be the result of extremely poor part writing by the arranger. Particularly with Barbershop music, diminished and augmented intervals in all parts are often used with indiscretion because the arranger is concentrating on chordal effects more than on good part writing. A course in *counterpoint* would be very good for such an arranger. Often a simple adjustment of chord parts will effect the solution.

Long Hold

Most amateur singers tend to run out of breath quickly. They have not learned to expand their chest cavities properly. They do not know how to employ deep breathing. Most often they are inefficient in their tonal production. Consequently, they may not be able to sustain a long phrase in one breath. If this is the case with your choir, you may want to study the phrases and mark more breath points. Do this only if the sense of the phrase can be maintained. The integrity of the word structure is most important. The meaning could be completely changed if you break up the phrase improperly.

It might be your desire to hold a single tone or produce a unified phrase beyond the ability of most of your singers to sustain because they may run out of breath quickly. There is a trick you can use to give you an endless possibility. The audience will never suspect. A long sustained tone, used judiciously, can be quite surprising to an audience. You will have to rely on the sensitivity of each individual in the chorus. First, have the group practice entering a pitch on the vowel very softly, breathing into the tone without scooping the pitch and without any starting "bump." After the soft start, have them crescendo to a forte. When they have learned to do this well, they will be ready for the next step.

Now, explain to the singers that they have the capacity to sense the reactions of the persons standing next to them. The purpose is to be able to hold a "chorus tone" indefinitely, irrespective of an individual's ability to sustain that tone. Encourage them to sense when their partner is about to take a breath and see to it that they do not take a breath at the same time. Tell them to arrange to take their breath either before or after the partner does. Be sure to come in exactly on pitch, breathe into the tone without any "bump," increase to proper volume, and then hold until after the next person takes his breath. It will take some practice to perfect the procedure, but the chorus will soon be able to maintain a beautiful dynamic balance if they can master alternate breathing.

Strain

A director should use both ears and eyes to constantly monitor his group. Instruments with small mouthpieces, such as trumpets and oboes, are apt to cause the player the earliest fatigue. Similarly, singers, most often the tenors and sopranos, whose parts take them consistently into the upper part of their vocal range will tire more quickly. Listen to the production of their tone quality. The first sign of strain may appear when the tone begins to sound scratchy or thin. Signs of hard breathing and more especially the appearance of strain in the neck muscles are immediate clues.

Before the performers reach the point of fatigue, you had better rest that section for a time. You can justify plenty of reasons to rehearse another section on difficult passages, the production of better tone quality, proper enunciation, attacks, releases, and so on until the first section has regained its competence. There is no need to tell anybody why you are doing this. If you tell them they look tired, they will be. If you don't mention it, they will feel refreshed and relaxed after the rest.

Planning

Study the music in your library to be sure it is easily within the capability of your group. You must cull out any impossible or too difficult numbers before you make a list of available pieces. Then go to a good music store or university library and critically select good, suitable music for your choir to replace the culled numbers.

Make a list, breaking it into several categories for quick reference...for example: fast, slow, rhythmic, or smooth; solos included; melodic or discordant; modern or baroque; and so on. If your group happens to be a church choir, you had better classify the text topics also so as to correspond and integrate with the pastor's sermons.

Develop a calendar to record the numbers for each rehearsal. Never throw too much at your choir at a time, but plan as far ahead as possible. When first introducing a new number, do not expect or demand perfection on the first or second reading. Like any new friend, it is necessary to get acquainted first. A true and lasting love is perfected over a long time.

If you are preparing for a concert, a variety of music should be your goal. An hour to an hour and a quarter is about all the concentration an audience can give. With an intermission, the concert will be about one and a half hours, which should be the maximum. Remember that an audience's appreciation of a concert lasts only as long as their posteriors can endure it. It is much better to do a great job on a short program and leave the audience wishing for more. If your program is too long, you may send them away, perhaps very much appreciating your excellence, but glad to get home. Enough of a good thing is sometimes too much.

If you are directing a church choir, your problem is somewhat different. Plan several months in advance, selecting topics according to the religious calendar of events. Alteration of your plan may be necessary occasionally to integrate with the pastor's pleasure, but in the main you will be in the ballpark. At rehearsals, it is best to concentrate on putting the finishing touches on next Sunday's composition, spend an adequate time perfecting the second Sunday's score, and then devote a small portion of the time on the third Sunday's program to get the choir acquainted with the piece. If your choir is expected to sing two numbers each Sunday, the same principle applies, but you might better select one easy number along with one a bit harder.

Christmas and Easter seasons often require extra music because of expanded Sunday and midweek services. Then it is necessary for you to plan far in advance and start your introductory run-through a month and a half to two months ahead. If you do this, you will not be faced with last-minute frustration. The choir will have gradually absorbed the musical content and be ready for the finishing touches in due time without dissatisfaction on either side, your's or the choir's.

The mind is retentive. As psychologists will tell you, a person "learns to roller skate in the winter and ice skate in the summer." This means that the mind while it is resting will unconsciously work on the details it has previously absorbed. The week between rehearsals gives the mind time for absorption, preparing it to be more receptive to refinement of detail. This is why you will be much less successful if you spend the entire rehearsal on only the number for the following Sunday. In the end you will have had to spend more time in the aggregate. Concentration of learning without an interval for absorption is not sufficient for amateurs.

Furthermore, no matter how much a singer may love the choir, there may be occasions when it will be impossible to attend a rehearsal. If you concentrate on rehearsing only one number each week, the singer will feel incompetent to sing that Sunday's number if the rehearsal was missed, and may not show up at all. If you have been practicing three or four weeks in advance, the singer can be confident about singing with the choir on any Sunday

CHAPTER XII

Exercise Techniques

Many trained directors prefer to start rehearsal with vocal exercises, all parts in unison. Quite often they will also add stretching exercises designed to limber up the chest and diaphragm muscles. Usually the director uses the first fifteen minutes of each rehearsal for such exercises.

A professional singer, preparing for a solo performance, appreciates the importance of such warmup before practicing and performing in order to develop stamina, increase the vocal range, and ensure more ease and proficiency. Amateur singers, on the other hand, are generally quite satisfied with their range and very much dislike too much expenditure of energy. The feeling of throat fatigue following vigorous exercises tends to spoil their enjoyment of the rest of the rehearsal.

Amateur singers come to a choir rehearsal primarily to participate in the joyful sound of good music and euphonious chords. Exercises sung in unison are not considered by most choir members as "good music," nor will they find in them anything harmonious to enjoy. Furthermore, unison exercises often take the sopranos and tenors too low and the altos and basses too high, which will strain and tire their voices before the director begins to practice selected music.

Monitor your group if you insist on exercises in unison. Begin a record of the number of singers who come to rehearsals fifteen minutes late. It is all right to try to determine why they are late and lend a sympathetic ear. However, they will hardly ever tell the truth to a direct question if they think the answer will displease you. Instead, they will usually give you the kind of excuse they think you will believe and accept. But your record will be a positive indication of their unwillingness to undergo the fatigue of your exercise procedure. If more and more singers appear late at your rehearsals, it is time for you to reconsider your plan. Either change your course or abandon it.

You might want to consider the following options. You can abandon the exercise period and substitute vocal exercises selected from phrases of the compositions you are working on. This can be accomplished near the beginning of your rehearsal time so, in effect, you will have gained your purpose more pleasantly than with unison exercises. The first two options are of this type.

Option I

Select an easy phrase from one of the compositions you are currently working on. If need be, use any excuse that may be plausible...to improve the intonation, to perfect attacks and releases, to smooth the passage by improving the uniformity of vowel sounds, or whatever will make good sense to the chorus.

Use the ay - ee - ah - oh - oo syllables; sing each chord slowly until absolutely satisfactory; change the rhythm as the various vowels are sung; make the singers watch your directing goals.

Option II

Polish up a hard passage. Your choir can very easily understand the necessity of practicing a difficult passage.

1. Use single vowels throughout the phrase to eliminate the complication of the words until the choir has mastered the music. If one section is having trouble, have them sing on the vowel while the other sections hum. Change the rhythm while singing on vowels only. Have the choir sing each chord slowly; do not move to the next chord until the preceding one is satisfactory. Sing the passage backward using a single vowel; increase the speed until the choir is totally familiar with the music of the passage.

2. Now sing the words; change the rhythm; if necessary, practice individual sections; relax half the choir by practicing two parts together in various combinations; make them listen to each other. Each section should be able to hear the other three sections clearly.

Option III

This third option can be used at the beginning of a rehearsal in place of unison exercises but with much more gratifying results.

Develop chordal exercises devised to adapt to your local needs and problems. If you have been a student of harmony and composition, you might do well to devise your own set of exercises to fit your group's needs. If you have been such a student, you will know that different chord positions, related to the tone in the bass, are called *inversions* of the chord. In a simple triad chord such as C-E-G, it is in the fundamental position if C is in the bass. If E is in the bass, it is the *first inversion*. If G is in the bass, it is the *second inversion*. Figure 44 makes this clear:

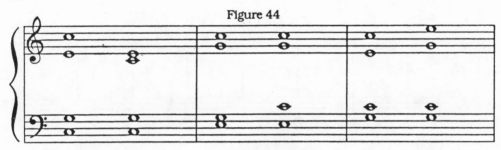

Figure 44

Fundamental   1st Inversion   2nd Inversion

You will note that in the first inversion of a major chord, the third of the chord appearing in the bass is most commonly *not* doubled or duplicated in any of the other parts. If you try such doubling, you will find the sonority very weak. About the only time you will find doubling the third permissible is when two parts, progressing in opposite directions, *momentarily* double the third. Figure 45 is an example.

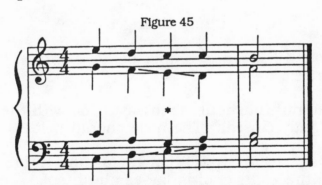

Figure 45

Seventh chords have three inversions and usually include all four tones in the chord. However, sometimes the fifth of the chord is omitted and the fundamental of the chord is doubled, which results in only a small reduction in sonority.

Particularly in Barbershop Harmony, the chords most often encountered are the major, the minor, the dominant seventh, the minor seventh, and the diminished seventh chords.

It is a good idea for quartets and choruses to vocalize practice exercises that include all these chords. By doing so, the singers learn to listen to one another and develop the proper "ring" on each chord. This will give you the opportunity to work on purity of vowel sounds at the same time.   Such practice also trains each singer to recognize the individual's position in each chord, making "free" harmonizing more flexible and enjoyable.

Figure 46
CHORD CHANGES

Figures 46 and 47 are examples of tuning and vocal techniques.   They are suitable for quartet or chorus use in close harmony.   You may need to revise the music portion of the examples to make them suitable for mixed chorus practice, but they are easy to adapt for that purpose.   For a men's chorus, the notes in the soprano clef are sung an octave lower.

Chord Changes

Figure 46 is an example of an exercise that uses chord changes.

1. Hum throughout (as in saying oo with the lips very tightly closed).   The nose should tickle.

2. Use various vowels one at a time throughout the entire eight chords (ay-ee-ah-oh-oo).

3. Use all vowels in sequence in *each* chord before proceeding to the next chord.

4. Move the diaphragm hard on each chord while saying ha-ha-ha-ha-ha (or ho-ho-ho-ho-ho), using such a rhythm as:

5. Use varying dynamics

6. Repeat at various pitch levels.

Figure 47
CHORD INVERSIONS

Chord Inversions

Figure 47 shows an exercise that uses chord inversions.

1. Sing ah-ah-ah-oh-oh-oh-ah (drop the jaw, move lips only to produce the vowels).

2. Sing ah-ah-ah-oo-oo-oo-ah (drop jaw as you progress higher, move lips only for different vowels).

3. Sing ay-ay-ay-ee-ee-ee-ay (drop jaw very wide on ee).

4. Practice varying rhythms.

   a. Each chord even.

   b.

5. Practice varying dynamics.
   a. Soft to loud.
   b. Loud to soft

c. Soft to loud to soft.
d. Loud to soft to loud.

6. Repeat at various pitch levels.

Figure 48
CHORDS IN POSITION

Chords in Position

To use chords in position as an exercise, See. Figure 48.

1. Use vowels suggested or use single vowel throughout.

2. Vary rhythm.

There is no end to the possibilities available to you if you have enough ingenuity and control of directing techniques. You will be most successful if you study your singers' individual preferences. Consult with them and listen to what they have to say. Then work around their prejudices to accomplish your purpose. There is no need to tell them all your thoughts and reasons. It is necessary only to give short and believable explanations about your plans and efforts to improve their singing—enough to pique their interest. You must, however, always maintain their confidence in your judgment.

Remember, it is the characteristic of *homo sapiens* to resist change. You must often move slowly, but surely, toward the proper end result, but amateurs are always delighted with accomplishment beyond their expectation. It is something of which they can be genuinely proud.

The suggestions given in this chapter relate to exercises in chordal context instead of the more common unison exercises. If you present them properly, a chorus will gain pleasure from creating good chordal harmony. They will feel the progress and more easily understand the beneficial results to be attained. Furthermore, their voices will not tire because each voice will be in range. And they will be forced to listen more closely to one another. They will enjoy the constant improvement in quality and balance that cannot be worked on when all are singing in unison. You will find that the members will be exceptionally well pleased when they are able to adjust their voices to ring true with each other. The sound of ringing chords will be a happy achievement for them.

CHAPTER XIII

Applied Techniques

For this chapter, I have selected two chorus numbers to exemplify practical conducting technique. The first, "Little Cowboy," has inherent in it a number of conducting problems characteristic of the treatment of any novelty song. The second, "The Lord's Prayer," has been selected because it combines more difficult conducting elements than most religious or even secular songs.

The "Little Cowboy" arrangement is for a male chorus. The tenors, with parts in the treble clef, will sing an octave lower than written. In performing such a song, it is imperative to employ sufficient rhythmic flexibility so that the words become effective. I hope this example will heighten your imaginative approach to a novel performance.

"The Lord's Prayer" will test your conducting skill, your knowledge of terminology, your use of both right and left-hand techniques that involve dynamic control, cueing, and many other considerations that I have analyzed for you.

If you are to be well prepared, you must analyze in detail all the musical problems in a score **before** the first rehearsal, spot trouble areas, decide on the exact conducting technique to apply at each point in a phrase, and completely absorb the music in all its aspects. The analysis of these two compositions is an example of the type of preparation required of any director when he first reviews a new composition. After diligent study and preparation, you need not fear the first rehearsal.

If you find any procedure you have tried to be ineffective, consider first exactly what you did, study the passage again, and determine whether you can possibly improve your technique. You are the leader. If the performers are not following your every indication exactly, more than likely your technique is at fault.

Study well the following examples measure by measure. If you master every element as I have explained it, you will be ready to apply the same principles to other compositions.

Figure 49

Little Cowboy—Meek

Figure 49

Novelty Songs

Several elements of novelty in producing an effect on an audience are common to most novelty songs;

1. An appealing story line.
2. Strong rhythm.
3. An element of surprise
4. Opportunity for chorus movement.
5. Use of special effects.

"Little Cowboy" was composed about thirty years ago; it was inspired by the antics of my four sons as they played together. All the novelty elements are possible to achieve with "Little Cowboy." My choruses have used it most successfully as an encore. Its special appeal seems to be that it reminds everyone of the antics of their own children or, for the younger people, the antics of their brothers and sisters or even themselves.

The tempo of the first verse should be slow enough for each word to be distinct and clear, yet move along with a positive and pronounced rhythm. The singers should be fully cognizant of the meaning of the words and register fun on their faces as they inspire the imagination of the audience with the spirit of a typical young lad.

In a song of this type, the words are more important than the music, so the phrasing will be dictated by its context. If you will recite the words of the first verse dramatically, you will find the need to pause briefly on the word "floor" at the phrase ending on "feet dragging on the floor." (See measure 4.)

Then, the pickup on "and" is emphasized and somewhat delayed to return to a rhythmic recital of "dismounting from his bike" and so on.

The elements of conducting this kind of interruption are shown in Figure 50. Direct the right hand through the first three beats in the normal manner, palm always facing the direction of the beat. Notice again that as the palm turns to a new direction, your hand will always make a loop.

Figure 50

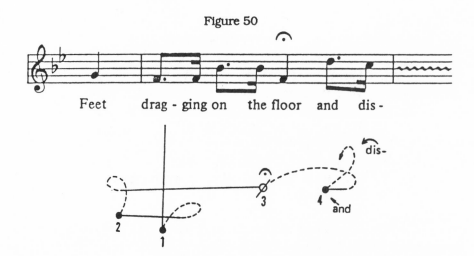

It is well to make the loop after beat two a little larger to cue the singers that you are going to hold beat three. Also a somewhat slower approach to point three is an additional cue. When you arrive in position at point three, you simply stop your hand movement entirely and hold (see the symbol ⌢).

Emphasize the word "and" as you would if you were reciting the words. Notice that no cutoff movement is necessary after holding the word "floor" because the loop movement to beat four will automatically accomplish the cutoff after the hold as well as cue the singers to take a breath during the progress of the loop. They will then be ready to attack the "and" as your palm turns to the point at beat four.

Another short pause at the point of beat four and the singers will sing and hold the "and" as long as you think appropriate. When ready, proceed to beat one in the ordinary manner. The singers will "feel" the sixteenth note on "dis-" and come in on "mounting" with you as you continue the original tempo.

The chorus starting with "Bang, bang, bang" should be strongly rhythmic until "the rustlers went kerplop" (*kerplop* being a favorite expression of my youngsters). At this point, give the chorus an adequate chance to breathe by making a larger-than-normal loop from beat three to beat four. The following word "but" should be held a full quarter count. Because you are exemplifying the words of the song, the phrase "but all I could hear was a *gentle* pop, pop" should naturally be sung softly.

The second verse can be very effective if one of the male singers has a dramatic voice. If so, let him stand forward and dramatically recite the words as the singers hum or sing on an appropriate vowel. The speaker should talk in oratorical style, using his hands and body to help express the words. He also could have two cap pistols stuck into his belt or holster.

For example, his hand can indicate the "mask o'er his face," draw the guns from his belt at "guns full drawn" while pointing from side to side as if the rustlers were really every place. When "he was about to leave" is reached, he replaces the guns as he steps leftward. Then, suddenly he turns his head to the right as he spies one more, his right hand pointing to the imaginary rustler. Both hands are thrown up in surprise and brought down to the knees as he "drops to the floor."

During the recitation, the singers produce an "oo" or "ah" in the original tempo but disregard the dotted eighths and sixteenths, singing only the basic harmony. Here is an excellent opportunity for the singers to sway left on beat one and right on beat three of each measure. In doing so, the general tendency is to bend at the knee and swing the hips only, which produces at best a minor effect. It is better for the singers to swing the torso above the hips as they put their weight on each leg alternately. This will move the shoulders left and right. Also, have them loosen their neck muscles so that the head can sway in each direction with the shoulder movement. This creates a very nice visual effect. You will find that the audience will react accordingly.

After singing the chorus for the second time, return to the third verse. The tempo should now reflect the attitude of a tired little boy. Use a slower tempo and lots of rubato at the end of each phrase until you have put him to "bed." Now, pick up the tempo again at "and in his dreams."

As you approach the ending of the third chorus, the orator again stands forward, draws his pistols, and fires his caps at "pop, pop" and again at the very end at the chorus cutoff.

What I have been discussing here is how a director can use imagination and employ flexibility to please an audience with a performance. In a novelty song, particularly, much liberty of interpretation is acceptable. In fact, in nearly every song of whatever type, the words should dictate the interpretation and phrasing. Make sure the words are pronounced properly and clearly. If the audience cannot understand the words, they will most likely not appreciate the music either.

Religious Songs

Figure 51

The Lord's Prayer—Malotte

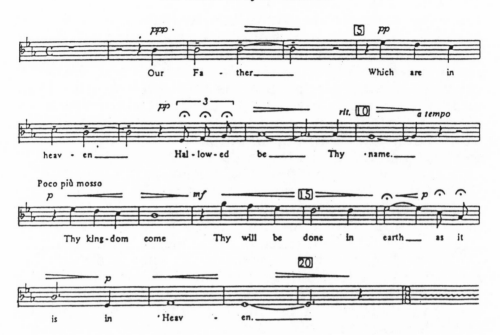

Malotte's "The Lord's Prayer is one of the loveliest choral compositions ever written. What a shame to allow it to be poorly performed! For the composition to be successfully beautiful, you must study in detail all the special nuances inherent in each phrase and pay particular attention to the relationship between the choral parts and the accompaniment. Malotte has signified, by musical indicators, the rubato phrasing and dynamics that must be followed carefully if the song is to be completely effective.

For the purpose of detailed analysis, let us study this composition in parts. Figure 51 shows the first 20 measures, which involve the 4/4 time signature (often marked with a "C").

Notice the instruction, "Lento, religioso." This means that the composition should be performed slowly and with deep religious feeling.

The song starts with an accompaniment in triplets. The accompaniment should slightly emphasize the first note of each triplet so that the singers can feel the rhythm. This is important because you will *not* beat out the rhythm but only nod or give the first beat to indicate to the accompanist that you are ready.

If you are not pleased with the accompanist's tempo, the rehearsal is the time to correct it. It should be *abso-*

lutely unnecessary for you to beat through the first measure and a half. The accompanist will probably ignore you anyway because it is a solo and will be played as the accompanist pleases. At the performance, it is too late to change the accompanist's tempo, but remember, in any case, the accompanist is probably as good a musician as you are.

The choral part starts on beat four. At the beginning of the second measure, place your hand in the position of beat three to inform the singers they are about to begin. When the accompaniment reaches beat three, you will start your rebound, looping to beat four positively, just as if you had actually produced beat three and had proceeded in the normal manner during a complete measure (see Figure 52).

Figure 52

Notice that the dynamic marking is "ppp" or "pianississimo," meaning very , very softly. It would be well for you to place your left hand in front of your chin or at your lips, palm toward the chorus, to indicate that they should start very softly.

Some music editors put a line over the half notes on "father" and "heaven." This usually means to elongate the beat value, but here, by interpretation, it means to give full value and to avoid singing the consonants "th" and "v" too soon. The decrescendo sign at the end of "father" means to get softer. Here it can mean only that the chorus will fade out on the end of the second beat of the fourth measure.

There are two acceptable methods of directing measures 3 and 4. The first way is to beat out the four beats in measure 3, and beat out the first two beats in measure 4, with a cutoff at beat three. If you like this method, you must notice that it is primarily important to emphasize beats one and three in measure 3, and beat one and the cutoff beat three in measure 4. The other beats are nearly superfluous because it is not necessary to direct the accompanist.

In measure 3 you will, therefore, make a definite beat on one, a very small beat on two, a large loop rebound to emphasize the approach to three, a small movement (or even a tap movement) on four, and a rebound again to the beat one in measure 4. Beat one, then, is positive, and beat two is a small movement followed by the loop rebound as a cutoff. Let the accompanist worry about beats three and four. Your responsibility is to the chorus. The pattern of these beats is shown in Figure 53.

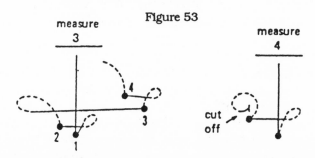

Figure 53

A second—and just as effective—way to conduct measures 3 and 4 is to indicate only the beats for "fa," "ther," and the cutoff. It is not necessary to indicate each beat. The chorus will *feel* the beats in the accompaniment anyway, particularly since the rhythm has already been established. As simple as it may seem, the chorus can easily follow your intent if you use the pattern of movements shown in Figure 54.

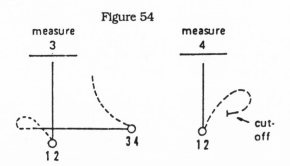

Figure 54

This can be done so long as there is no chord movement from the last of measure 3 through the cutoff in measure 4.

Having signaled the cutoff, hold your hand still in place. When the accompanist reaches beat one in measure 5, produce a rebound to beat two for the chorus to come in on the word "which," continuing through beats three and four to beat one on "heav-." Eliminate beat two, rebound to beat three on "en," and also eliminate beat four. Here, however, it is different from measure 4, because measure 7 changes the chord. See the asterisk above measure 7. Instead of holding, as in the first phrase, it now is necessary to indicate beat one in measure 7, then hold to the cutoff on beat three. You should have noticed also that measures 5 through 7 are slightly louder, a "pp" or pianissimo instead of "ppp."

In measure 7, beat three, the accompanist comes in on the rest. The fermatas over each of the triplets on the word "Hallowed" mean that you should elongate each triplet to the equivalent of three quarter notes. After the cutoff on "heaven" and the chord on beat three, conduct these triplets exactly as you directed measure 5's quarter notes on the words "which art in" (as if they were really beats two, three, and four).

You now come to beat one in measure 8. Hold through measure 9 while your left hand indicates a gradual softness—indicated by the ⟶ which means decrescendo. On beat three of measure nine, rebound as if you had just approached a three beat, palm to right. Turn your palm for a loop to beat four on the word "thy." Note the word "rit" (for "ritard") above "thy," which indicates that the accompaniment triplets are to be elongated, lengthening the word "thy." Then return to tempo (a tempo) on the word "name." Hold on the first beat of measure ten and use the cutoff on beat two of measure eleven.

At this point we find the instruction "poco più mosso" which means to increase the tempo, or go faster gradually. The accompanist will set this new tempo. Pick up "Thy Kingdom come" in the same manner as in measure five. However, the difference is the crescendo/diminuendo in measures twelve and thirteen. The phrase is marked with a single "p" or "half-voice." Use your left hand to tell your singers to grow louder. Turn the palm up, arm rising, and then turn the palm over, point downward, lowering your arm to indicate they are to grow softer. The right hand will have held the four beats on the word "come," and the cutoff is on beat one at the rest in measure fourteen.

Now, an "mf" dynamic mark indicates a full voice and is followed by a crescendo/diminuendo. But notice the decrescendo on the word "done" to a "p" or soft, growing immediately back to "mf" on "earth." Hold beat one in measure 16 two counts, and rebound by turning your palm to the right on beat three because of the chord change. It is not necessary to beat the two because the chorus is not *moving*.

The words "as it" have fermatas or holds over each eighth note, so they must be elongated. Here, it is easiest to rebound from the third beat on "earth" to conduct "as" as a downbeat and "it" as an upbeat just as if it were a 2/8 beat coming down again in measure 17 for beat one on the word "is" (see Figure 55).

Figure 55

Measure 18 has a chord change on beat three that must be indicated along with a left-hand crescendo movement. Then hold measures 19 through 20, with a left-hand decrescendo and cutoff on beat 4.

Now, we will analyze the second half of "The Lord's Prayer" from measure 21 to the end of the composition (see Figure 56). Notice that the time signature has changed from 4/4 to 9/8, that is from four quarter notes a measure to nine eighth notes a measure. The basic tempo, however, has not changed, so you should go from a four-beat measure to a three-beat measure. This results in the 9/8 time being directed in triplets, three eighth notes to a beat.

You have just cutoff the chorus on measure 20. Now leave it up to the accompanist to play the next four measures without your help—unless, of course, you want to risk having to follow the player instead of having the player follow you. Your responsibility is to the chorus, so you should stand still until the third beat of measure 24. Now, make the preliminary beat on beat three, and the chorus will start with you on beat one of measure 25.

Start beating three to a measure, the left hand indicating the very soft "pp" at "daily" with crescendo/diminuendo on "bread." Do *not* try to indicate the triplet division in measure 28 on the words "and for-." Give a strong three beat, and let the singers feel the eighth-note triplets. If you try to indicate the triplets, it will only be confusing and awkward and will accomplish nothing.

Measure 29 has the indication "poco accel.," meaning a "little increase in speed," as well as another crescendo and diminuendo in measure 30. If you have the chorus sing "trespasses," you may want to direct beat two. But if you have them sing "debts," it is unnecessary because there is no chord movement. Here you can accomplish the chord hold from beat one to beat two, cut the singers off and bring them in on beat three quite easily, shown in Figure 57.

Figure 56

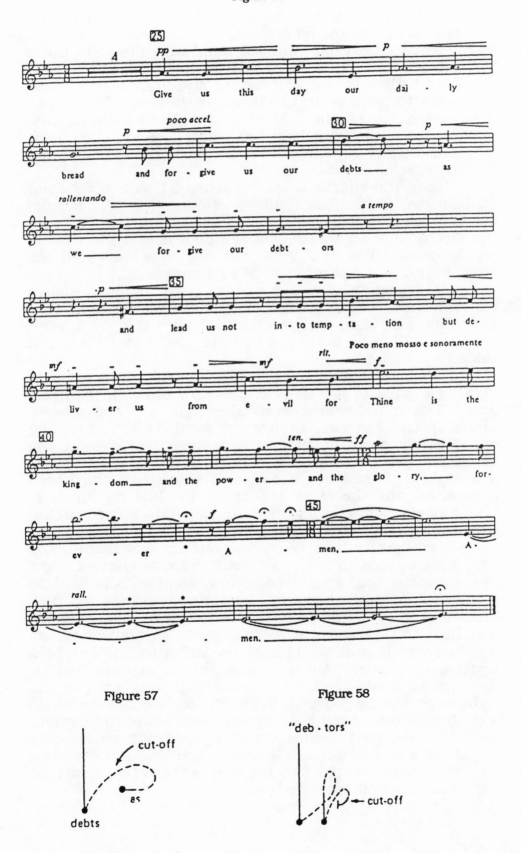

Figure 57

Figure 58

Make a regular downbeat, hold to beat two, turn your palm to the right, and make a cutoff loop by turning your wrist and palm through the loop to beat three on the word "as." At the same time, raise your left hand with the palm up to indicate a crescendo to beat one on the word "we." Note the word "rallen-tan-do," meaning gradually slower, coupled with the descrescendo through the word "debt-ors." It is easiest to conduct "debt-ors" with two downbeats. This makes a cutoff on beat two easier (see Figure 58). It is not necessary to conduct beat three. The accompanist has the next phrase.

Bring the chorus in on measure 34 with a rebound off beat two to "pop" beat three. Notice the "p" marking, the crescendo/diminuendo on measures 35 and 36, and the strong beat on three. Let the chorus feel the triplets on the words "but de-." Now you will have indicated the move to "mf" and the move to "f" in measure 39.

At this point are the words "poco mene mosso, e sonoramente," which mean a little less motion and very sonorous, full, rich, and resonant. Notice the word "ten." (for "tenuto"), which means to hold and sustain for full value.

At measure 42, the time signature changes again to 12/8. Go back to a four-beat measure but still in triplet form. This is the climax with "ff" on "glo-ry." Measure 44 needs special analysis. Notice the word "ev-er" where the chord changes on the first beat in measure 44 (note the asterisk). You must direct and hold that first beat. This is a complicated measure because of the holds, the chord movement, and the extra pickup on the last eighth note. The way you direct this measure depends somewhat on which words your chorus uses.

If you prefer "and ev-er. A-," you are now holding the first beat of measure 44. Pretend to draw another leger line between "and" and "ever." Now, come off the hold as if the next downbeat were on the dotted half note on "ev-." The "and" is produced by a rebound loop as if it were the last beat of the measure proceeding to the downbeat on "ev-." There is a chord change on "er" with another hold or fermata. To indicate this, after the strong one-beat on "ev-," make a small rebound by turning your wrist to the right to produce a move as if the "er" on the chord change were beat three. Then hold again. Because of the fermata over the "A-" just before the 9/8 time signature, that eighth note should get a full beat value. So, after holding the "er," turn your palm to the left as if producing a beat four. Then turn it to a one-beat on "-men."

Figure 59

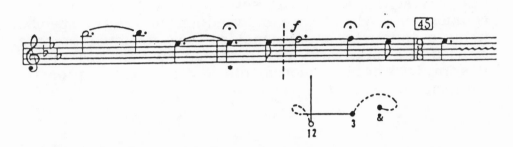

If you prefer the optional "for-ev-er-. A-men" you will direct basically the same way, with the main difference being a cue in with the left hand on the last eighth note in the upper two parts only. The eighth note on "and" does not appear in this option as it does in the first option. After holding beat one to finish off the word "ev-er," move your right hand up again just as you would with a preparatory beat to one and make a one-beat on "A-." Rebound as if going to beat three on the chord change, and hold the fermata.

Now, the two higher parts (in a men's chorus, the tenors) will come down on the last eighth note, which also has a fermata. At this point, hold your right hand still. Use eye-to-eye contact with the tenors, cue them in with the left hand, the right hand still holding the baritones and basses. Now, raise both hands together on a preliminary beat to one in measure 45.

Figure 60

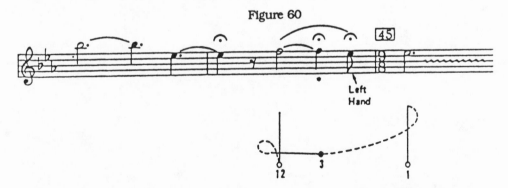

At measure 45, return to 9/8 time in the original tempo with a "mf" dynamic and decrescendo. In measure 46, you must cue in the third beat, with your left hand indicating soft, or "p." Notice the further decrescendo to very soft, or "pp," and the "rall." indication for "rallentando," or gradual slowing and broadening of the last three, moving, dotted quarter notes.

There are other methods of producing detailed conducting techniques in the several critical areas of this composition. What I have analyzed for you are the specific items a conductor must consider, how he must prepare himself to attain clarity and precision, and the technicalities involved in hand movements to communicate properly with the singers.

CHAPTER XIV
Terminology

NOTATION

Staff

A staff consists of five parallel lines upon which are placed clef signs and key signatures to determine the pitch of each line.

Ledger or Leger Lines

Each line of the staff is called a ledger line. Additional ledger lines may be added above or below the staff to extend and accommodate additional notes beyond the range of the staff.

Figure 61

Measure

A staff is divided into portions by placing perpendicular bars on it. The space between the bars is called a measure.

Figure 62

Clef

A clef sign appears at the beginning of each line of the staff to indicate the intended pitch of the notes on the staff. The use of clef signs is easy to understand if you consider the treble and bass staffs to be connected by a ledger line on middle C. This eleven-line staff is sometimes called the "Great Staff."

Figure 63

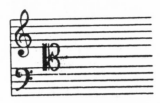

Treble Clef

The curl of the treble symbol wraps around the line that designates G above middle C. It is used by soprano and alto singers and higher-pitched instruments. In men's choruses, it is understood that the notes for tenors as written on the treble staff will be sung an octave lower. Some composers and arrangers use a double symbol to indicate the tenor parts.

Because of the position of the curl, the clef sign is sometimes called the G clef. The pitches on each line, starting at the bottom line, are E, G, B, D, F, which is easily remembered by using the mnemonic phrase, "**E**very **G**ood **B**oy **D**oes **F**ine." The names of the spaces between the lines are easily remembered, also. From the bottom space upward, in order, they spell "**FACE.**"

Figure 64

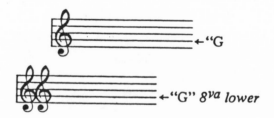

Alto or Tenor Clef

The break in the symbol for the alto or tenor clef indicates the position of middle C on the staff, which accounts for the name "C clef," which it is sometimes called. It is considered by many to be a "movable" clef sign because the ledger lines seem to vary. But, in reality, because the clef sign always designates middle C, it is the associated lines of the staff that are movable.

Figure 65

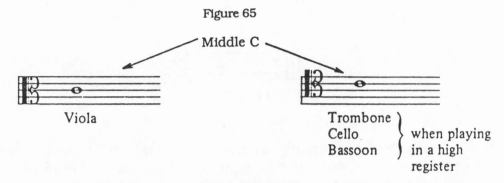

Bass Clef

The bass clef symbol curves around F below middle C, the F being delineated by two dots. This clef is used for the lower-voiced singers and low-pitched instruments, including the tenor voices in a mixed chorus.

Figure 66

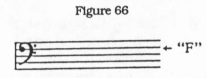

Practical Conversions

Notice that the four lower lines of the bass staff have the same names as the four upper lines of the treble staff. The two staves relate by the interval of one third, plus an octave.

The relationship between the alto C clef staff and the treble staff is useful in converting a violinist into a viola player. The violin is tuned to G, D, A, E. The upper three strings of the viola are identical to the violin's lower three strings, G, D, A, with the fourth string an octave below middle C, thus tuned to C, G, D, A.

The fourth line on the treble staff, D, can be played on the violin with the first finger on the A string in the *third* position.

Figure 67

The fourth line on the alto staff is E, which on the viola is played with the first finger on the D string in the *first* position.

Figure 68

"D" string

1st finger

Both the A string on the violin and the D string on the viola are third strings from the bottom. Therefore, a violinist can learn to play the viola quite quickly by playing the viola in the first position with the same relative fingering as would be used in the same staff location while playing the violin in the third position.

Time Signatures

The numbers following the clef sign at the beginning of a composition, or at a change that occurs during the progress of the work, indicate the rhythmic character within the measure. The numbers are called the *time signature* . The upper number gives the number of beats in each measure. The lower number gives the type of note which is to get one beat. For example:

4/4 time = four quarter notes per measure, a quarter note equaling one beat. Sometimes indicated by a "C," which means 4/4.

Figure 69

2/4 time = two beats per measure with a quarter note equaling one beat.

Figure 70

6/8 time = six beats per measure, an eighth note equaling one beat. However, if the tempo is fast, conduct in two beats, which results in two groups of triplets, each triplet comprising one beat.

Figure 71

3/4 time = three beats per measure, a quarter note to a beat.

Figure 72

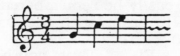

12/8 time = twelve beats to the measure, an eighth note equaling one beat. If the tempo of the composition is very rapid, direct in three or four rather than twelve, depending upon the rhythmic accents. This will result in four eighth notes to a beat (quadruplets) or three eighth notes to the beat (triplets).

Figure 73

2/2 time (often called "alla breve") = two half notes to the measure. Sometimes indicated by "¢" and called "cut-time."

Figure 74

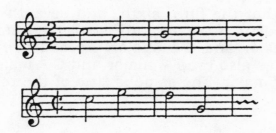

Key Signatures

Symbols given at the beginning of each staff to indicate the scale and key of the composition are called key *signatures*. The same key signature may indicate either a major or a minor key (or sometimes a modal key). A sharp (♯) raises a tone one half step. A flat (♭) lowers a tone one half step. It is easy to remember the **sharps** in their order by memorizing the phrase "**F**ive **C**ats **G**ot **D**inner **A**t **E**d **B**rown's," in which the first letter of each word indicates this order of the sharps—F♯, C♯, G♯, D♯, A♯, E♯, B♯.

The flats can easily be remembered in a similar way. The first four flats in order spell the word "**BEAD**." The last three flats can be recalled by the first letter of the words "**G**ood **C**lothes **F**it." Thus, you have B♭ E♭, A♭, D♭, G♭, C♭, F♭ in order by using the phrasing above . If you have memorized the sharps in their order, the names of the related major keys are always just a half step above the last sharp named. Thus, one sharp in the key signature is the key of G major, which is a half step above the first sharp, F ♯. The key of E major has four sharps, the last sharp being half a step below the key name, or "D ♯." Therefore, the key of E has four sharps—F♯, C♯, G♯, D♯.

When considering the names of the major keys having flats, the major key name is always the same as the next-to-last flat. Consider B♭ E♭ A♭ D♭ G♭ C♭ F♭ as a continuous circle. Then, F♭ will precede B♭ . So, with one flat, the next-to-last flat will be F♭ , but notice that in this case the key of F will be F♮. All the others will bear the flat as part of their key name. A key in one flat would then indicate the major key of F, and a key signature with four flats would be A♭ major.

The designation of major keys is usually given by using a capital letter, whereas the minor keys are usually indicated by a small letter. The minor keys are related to the corresponding major keys by being a minor third lower. In the circle of keys below, the capital letters indicate the major keys and the lowercase letters, the corresponding minor keys.

Notice that the fifth, sixth, and seventh sharp keys are the equivalent of the seventh, sixth, and fifth flat keys. That is, B major and C♭ major are called *enharmonic equivalents*, as also are F♯ major and G♭ major, and C♯, major and D♭ major. The same is true of the related minor keys.

This circle of keys has been in use for more than 200 years. It is a most convenient tool for the student and the musical theorist. It is interesting that our present day Barber-shop Singers and arrangers use this same system. Instead of designating the true key names, however, they have assigned numbers to the elements of the circle and make the claim that they have something very different, a modern innovation.

Figure 75

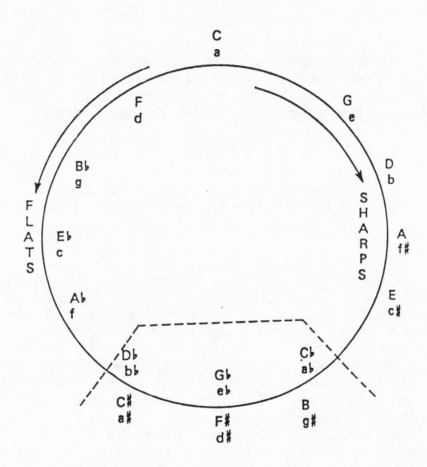

Accidentals

During the course of a composition, incidental pitch changes may be desirable or, through modulation, a whole phrase might be written in a different key. It then is necessary to indicate alterations in the original key signature as the composition progresses. Such changes are called *accidentals* .

An accidental may consist of the sharp or flat previously explained or a double sharp, (𝕏) which raises a tone two half steps or a double flat (♭♭), which lowers a tone two half steps.   A natural (♮) appears **only** as an accidental, cancelling any sharp, flat, double sharp, or double flat either in the key signature or a prior accidental within a specific measure.   Any accidental is strictly limited to its particular line on the staff, that is, it does not affect notes an octave above or below that staff line and is effective for the duration of only that one measure.

Bars

Single bars divide a staff into measures. A double bar, with two thin lines, indicates the end of a section of the composition. A double bar with one thin line followed by a heavy line indicates the end of the composition.

Figure 76

Section

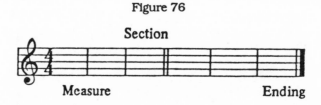

Measure   Ending

A double line, one thin and the other heavy, when combined with two dots indicates a repeat. A heavy line to the right, the thin line with the two dots to the left, means to repeat back to a similar sign reversed, i.e. with the dots and thin line appearing to the right. If the words "da capo" (DC) or "dal segno" (DS) appear above the repeat symbol, it is not necessary to indicate the reversed line and dot repeat sign. "Da capo" (from the head) over the repeat sign means to go back to the head or beginning of the composition. If "dal segno" (from the sign 𝄋) appears, it means to go back to the symbol 𝄋 . Then you will repeat the music usually using second endings only.

Figure 77

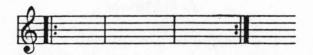

The final repeat bar is often accompanied by indications for a first and second ending. The bracket above the measures just preceding, marked ⌐1   ⌐, indicates the ending measures to be performed the first time through. Having accomplished the repeat, skip the indication for the first ending and proceed to the measures following the repeat bar, which will be marked .

Figure 78

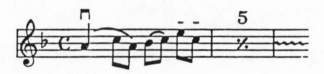

Another symbol sometimes placed between measure bars means to repeat the previous measure as is. If it is to be repeated a number of times, often the number of measures to be consecutively repeated will appear at the top of the measure.

Figure 79

Rests

A rest is a rhythmic silence in music. Following is a table that shows the types of rests and the equivalent notes.

Equivalent Note	Name	Rest	Description
⧈	Double Whole note (breve)	⊦	Whole measure rest, hangs down from 4th ledger line.
○	Whole note= 4 (semibreve)	▬	Whole rest, hangs down from 4th ledger line.
♩	Half note = 2 (minim)	▬	Half rest. Lies above middle line.
♩	Quarter note = 1 (crotchet)	⅃	Quarter rest, placed across center ledger line.

♪   Eighth note (quaver)   ɣ   Eighth rest

♬   Sixteenth note (semi-quaver)   ᵧ   Sixteenth rest

♬   Thirty-second note (demisemi-quaver)   ⅔   Thirty-second rest.

Dotted Notes

A dot following a note increases the value of that note by a half. Thus, a half note with a dot (𝅗𝅥.) has the value of three quarter notes. A dotted eighth note is equivalent to an eighth note plus a sixteenth note. It is not customary to place a dot after any rest. Rests occur only in combination.

Note	*Equivalent*	*Rests*
𝅗𝅥.	𝅗𝅥 ◡ 𝅘𝅥	▬ 𝄽
𝅘𝅥.	𝅘𝅥 ◡ ♪	𝄽 ɣ
♪.	♪ ◡ ♬	ɣ ᵧ

Slur

A line over two or more notes of *different pitches* indicates that the included notes are to be played legato, or smoothly. For string players, a slur is an indication that the included notes are to be played in one direction of the bow. Sometimes the slur will simply indicate melodic phrasing. (See figure 80).

Figure 80

Tie

A tie is an indication that two notes of the *same pitch* should be played for the duration of their *combined* values as one tone. The tie connects the heads of the notes.

Figure 81

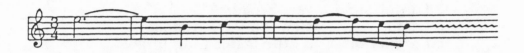

Octaves

The symbol "8va" is often used to indicate that the note or series of notes is to be played an octave higher or lower (bassa). If there is a series of notes in the pattern, a bracket may be added for the extent of that phrase.

Figure 82

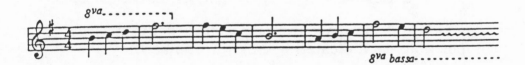

TEMPO

Tempo means rate of speed. The tempo instructions are not absolutely specific although an established normal tempo is agreed upon within general limits. A certain freedom of choice exists with slight variations left up to the pleasure of the performer.

A chosen tempo on a particular performance may be affected by many things, such as whether the auditorium is large or small, whether the audience seems lively or fatigued, or simply how the performer happens to feel at that moment. For these and many other reasons, every performance will be different from any previous performance. Knowing this, composers often write metronome instructions, for instance, ♩ = c. 132, (ie. 132/min.), the "c" standing for the Latin "circa" meaning "around". Sometimes the metronome instruction is ♩ = c. 120—132, meaning "take your pick within these limits." If the speed is to change during the progress of the composition, the composer may indicate a new tempo mark. If the first tempo is to return again, "Tempo I" or "Tempo primo" might be indicated.

Gradual changes in tempo, as indicated by such directions as "ritardando" or "accelerando," may be followed by the words "a tempo," which also means to return to the basic tempo. The following directions are most common at the beginning of a movement:

Grave:	slow, heavy, solemn.
Larghissimo:	very broad.
Largo:	slow, stately, broad.
Larghetto:	a little faster than largo.
Lento:	slow.
Adagio:	slow, leisurely.
Adagietto:	slightly faster than adagio.
Andante:	in a walking tempo, moderately slow.
Andantino:	a little faster than andante.
Moderato:	moderately (= c. 80).
Allegretto:	rather fast, fairly lively.
Allegro:	fast cheerful.
Vivace:	lively, spirited.
Presto:	quick, rapid, very fast.
Prestissimo:	extremely fast, as fast as possible.

Gradual changes in tempo during the course of a composition are indicated by such words as the following:

Retardando (Rit.):	slackening, gradually slower.
Ritenuto:	hold back, slower.
Accelerando:	quickening, to increase gradually, go faster.
Ad Libitum :	at liberty, allowing the
(ad lib.)	performer to vary the strict tempo at pleasure.

These instructions are usually followed by "a tempo" to indicate where to return to the original tempo.

DYNAMICS

Dynamics are the gradation of intensity in the sound of the music. The interpretation of a marking that indicates the dynamics, may depend entirely upon the gradation of intensity of the passage just preceding it. For instance, if the preceding passage was very soft, then a moderate increase in intensity can give the effect of a much louder increase because of the contrast. If the passage was moderately loud instead, then much more increase may be necessary to give the same relative effect. It is also important for the composer and the conductor to know well the timbre of different instruments. The violin section may have to be marked medium loud, but the trumpet may have to be marked soft in order to prevent the trumpets from overriding the violins.

Crescendo

A "crescendo" is a gradual increase in loudness or intensity, indicated by "cresc." or the symbol ——————— .
The word comes from the Italian, meaning "increasing." It was used first in Italian opera scores in the early 18th century. Instruments that are struck by hammers, such as the piano and the tympani, affect a crescendo by repeating each note, successively hitting each one a little harder. String, woodwind, and brass instruments and voices have the capacity of sustaining a tone and, therefore, may vary the intensity during the progress of the tone. A crescendo is often indicated more precisely, by adding dynamic markings such as p ◁————ff.

Figure 83

DECRESCENDO and DIMINUENDO: The terms "decrescendo" and "diminuendo" indicate a gradual decrease in loudness or intensity. These words are often abbreviated "decresc.," "dimin.," or "dim.," or by the symbol ——————▷ . To be more specific, the dynamic direction may be marked as *ff* ——————— *mf* or p ———————▷ *ppp*.

PIANISSIMO: Pianissimo the superlative of the instruction "piano," indicated by "pp," meaning very soft. Some composers tend to abuse instructions to the extent of writing "pppp" to impress the performer to play as softly as possibly.

PIANO: "Piano" a direction to the performer to play softly. It is indicated by the mark "p".

MEZZOPIANO: "Mezzopiano" is derived from the Latin "medius," meaning "middle." In music, mezzo means medium, moderate, or half. Mezzopiano, therefore, means medium soft or half loud, or in other words, moderately soft. It is abbreviated "mp."

MEZZOFORTE: "Mezzoforte" means moderately loud, half way between mezzopiano (medium soft) and forte (loud). It is abbreviated "mf."

FORTE: "Forte" is derived from the Latin "fortis," meaning "strength," a direction to the performer to play loud and strong. Its abbreviation is "f." Since the Romantic Period of music, composers have taken to writing "ff" (fortissimo) and "fff" or "ffff" to encourage the performer to greater effort. Forte is not specific as to actual intensity. It means only to produce tones that give a feeling of loudness.

FORTE-PIANO: The abbreviation "fp," for "loud-soft," means to start loud, then immediately become soft. The symbol sometimes is used incorrectly to indicate an accent. The dynamic marking is sometimes reversed. "Pf" or "piano-forte" was first used before 1800, when the modern piano became the first keyboard instrument capable of varying the dynamic from soft to loud as opposed to instruments such as the harpsichord.

SFORZANDO and SFORZATO: From the Italian, "sforzare" meaning "to force." In music, it means to accent with sudden force or emphasis, that is, with a strong accent on a single note or chord. It is sometimes combined with other terms—for example, "sf-p," which means to accent and follow immediately with soft. These terms are usually abbreviated "sfz."

SMORZANDO: "Smorzando" means that a note or phrase is to "die away."

INSTRUCTIVE TERMS

AD LIBITUM: as you please, freely.

AFFETTUOSO: expressively, tenderly

AGITATO: agitated, fast, with excitement.

A LA, ALLA: at the, to the, in the style or manner of.

Al FINE: to the end.

A MEZZO VOCE: with half voice

ANIMATO: with spirit, animated.

APPASSIONATO: passionately.

ARCO: an instruction to the string player to resume playing with the bow.   Usually after a pizzicato (plucking) instruction.

A TEMPO: return to the previous rate of speed.

ATTACCA: play what follows without pause.

CANTABILE: song-like, easy, flowing

COL LEGNO: to bounce on the string with the wooden back of the string player's bow.

CON: with, by, to.

CON FUOCO: with fire.

CON MOTO: with motion.

CROTCHET: British for quarter note.

DETACHÉ: broad, vigorous stroke applied to single notes that are usually of equal value. Sometimes indicated with a line over or under the notes.

ENCORE: again, once more; a repetition or further performance in answer to audience applause.

FINE: end of a composition or the close of a repeated passage.

GIOCOSO: playfully, gay.

GIUSTO: strict, exact.

GRANDIOSO: elegantly, gracefully, smoothly.

LEGATO: smoothly, connected, with even style.

LOCO: play in place (usually after 8va).

MAESTOSO: majestic, stately, grand, dignified.

MA NON TROPPO: but not too much.

MARTELÉ or MARTELLATO: a severe staccato like a hammer stroke.

MEN or MENO: less

MEZZO: half, middle, medium.

MUTE: any of various devices to soften or muffle the tone of an instrument or an instruction to subdue the intensity of the tone by employing such a device on the bridge of a string instrument or in the bell of a brass instrument.

NON: not.

PIÙ: more; used in conjunction with other directions.

PIZZICATO (pizz.):   a direction to string players to pluck the string with the finger instead of bowing. It is usually done while holding the bow in the palm and doing the plucking with an extended finger. Sometimes, if the bow is occupied at the same time in playing alternate notes, the third and fourth fingers of the left hand will be used.

POCO: little: used in conjunction with other directions

POMPOSO: with dignity, pompously.

PRIMO: upper part, as the first part in a duet.

RAPIDO: rapidly.

RELIGIOSO: in a devotional style.

RINFORZANDO: sudden crescendo made prominent.

RISOLUTO: resolute, determined.

RUBATO: stolen time, to perform with regulated rhythmic freedom, using tones arbitrarily lengthened or shortened, that is, robbing the duration of some beats and adding to others.

SEC: produce a dry sound.

SECONDO: the second or lower part, as in a duet.

SEGNO: a sign (𝄋) at the beginning of a repeat.

SEMPLICE: with simplicity.

SEMPRE: always, without varying.

SENZA: without.

SERIOSO: seriously.

SORDINO: indicates to use a mute.

SOSTENUTO: sustained, sometimes at a slower tempo, each note to be held full value.

SOTTO: under, beneath.

SOTTO VOCE: half voice, an undertone hardly to be heard.

SOURDINE: mute, especially for the trumpet.

SPICCATO: a short stroke in rapid tempo, the passage   usually played by string players bouncing the bow on the string. Most often marked with dots at each note head.

SPIRITOSO: witty, humorously.

STACCATO: detached, separated, producing a slight pause between the melodic tones. Will produce a dry, light effect giving a contrast to legato playing. If a long passage is to be played staccato, the composer may write "sempre staccato" on the score. Usually marked with dots at head of the notes or, for a stronger effect, a martele marking.

STRINGENDO: hurried, accelerated, especially toward a climax.

SUBITO: suddenly, abruptly.

TACET: to be silent for an indicated time.

TENUTO: hold to full value, sustain, usually indicated by a short line over or under a note or chord.

TROPPO: too much, as in "Adagio ma non troppo," which means slowly but not too slowly.

VIGOROSO: with energy, vigorous.

VIVACE: brisk, lively, spirited.

CHAPTER XV

Choral History

A chorus or a choir, which is a chorus that sings in a religious service, customarily means any group of singers with more than one singer on a part. The name is derived from ancient Greece. In their plays, the "choros" was a group that danced and chanted comments during the course of the play.

Choral music has been written about almost every subject and has been performed on almost every occasion. It may be a simple arrangement of a folk tune or a highly complicated contrapuntal composition.

Choral singing is extremely popular. Male choruses, women's choruses, and mixed choruses appear in schools as a cappella choirs and glee clubs, in churches and synagogues as choirs, in corporate choruses, and in community choruses. The singing is in a variety of dedicated styles from Barbershop Harmony, cowboy songs, and ethnic songs to cantatas and oratorios.

Choral music has always been an important segment of religious services, beginning with works based on the words of the Catholic Mass as early as the 14th century. Some of the world's greatest musical masterpieces are the masses written by Palestrina in the 16th century and those of Bach, Mozart, Beethoven, Berlioz, and Verdi in later years. Add to these the beautiful oratorios by Handel and the cantatas and passions of Bach. Choruses have added excitement and color to many operas and operettas and have even been added to the scores of symphonies such as Mahler's Eighth Symphony, Stravinsky's Symphony of Psalms, and Beethoven's famous Ninth Symphony.

Most choral music is written to be sung in four parts: a mixed chorus with soprano, alto, tenor, and bass; a women's chorus with first and second soprano and first and second alto; or a men's chorus with first and second tenor and first and second bass. Glee clubs, Barbershop singers, and the like are more likely to designate the four part men's voices as top tenors, leads, baritones, and basses.

The Soprano

Soprano is the name given to the voice with the highest pitch, ranging from below middle C to as high as F, two-and-a-half octaves higher. However, the average amateur soprano will do well to reach a high A or approximately one-and-three-fourths octaves. Those sopranos with light and sweet voices are usually called lyric sopranos and are at their best when singing beautiful simple melodies. Others have big, rich-sounding voices and are called dramatic sopranos. The rarest is the coloratura soprano who is able to sing highly embellished melodies, able to trill like a bird and to sing as nimbly as a flute.

Figure 84

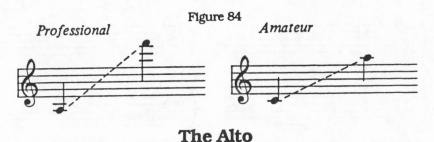

The Alto

The alto is in the lower of the natural ranges of women's voices. "Alto" in Italian means "high," so that the modern usage of the word has obviously changed. Originally, in medieval music, the tenor voice was given the melody, whereas the voice singing above it was called "alto" because it was higher. A man singing top tenor is now technically called a countertenor.

A professional alto may often have a two-and-a-half octave range usually from E below middle C to approximately high C, whereas an amateur's range is usually limited to G below middle C to high E, about an octave and a half.

Figure 85

The Tenor

The tenor is the highest of the natural adult male voices. In medieval music the tenor was the voice which carried or "held" the cantus firmus (or melody around which the other voices were written). The word "tenor" comes from the Latin "tenere," which means "to hold."

The tenor voice of an amateur usually ranges two octaves from C below middle C. It can sometimes be expanded higher by the use of falsetto, the false or artificial voice that lies above the tenor's natural voice. A professional singer can move through his falsetto unnoticeably, maintaining the same quality. Amateurs will often sing top tenor parts entirely in falsetto. The customary tenor range is as follows:

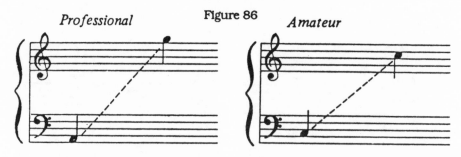

Figure 86

The voice selected for top or first tenor in a men's group is generally more flexible in the higher range and of lighter quality. The lead, or second, tenor is generally fuller voiced, rich and sonorous, and usually is used to carry the melody.

The Baritone

The majority of men speak and sing in a high bass voice called "baritone." It can be as agile as any other voice, as you might notice in the cantatas of Bach or the operas and oratorios of Handel. The same designations often apply to men's voices as to the high women's voices. For example, the light, flexible quality might refer to a "lyric" baritone or the full, sonorous voice might be called "dramatic." The ranges approximate the following:

Figure 87

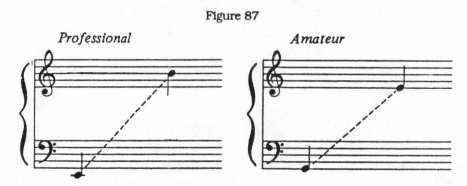

The Bass

The bass is the lowest voice part in music. Its part is most often the foundation upon which the other harmonic voices are written. A musical shorthand was developed in the 17th century that consisted of merely writing the bass part (called a "continuo") and placing numbers above the notes. This practice gave rise to the term "figured bass," a term now used mainly by theory students. Back then, however, instrumentalists as well as the vocalists would fill in the required tones by reading the chord numbers. The director, probably very familiar with the composition by rote training, would guide and correct the singers and instrumentalists in their harmony and melody.

A true bass voice is quite rare, being able to reach very low tones and having a deep, rich quality. In choral ensemble writing, the composer rarely writes for bass singers either as high or as low as when writing for solo performances.

In opera, the bass singer is rarely the romantic hero. Often he is a regal personage, a noble character, a lordly god, or sometimes the villain or comic character. He is usually given very long, low notes to sing to bring out the grave quality of the voice. If his range is exceptionally low, he is typified as a "basso profundo." Typical bass ranges are:

Figure 88

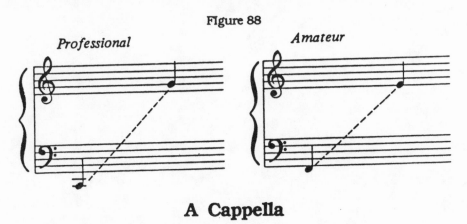

A Cappella

From the Italian, the term "a cappella" means "in chapel style." Notice that the word is spelled with two "p;s" and two "l's." Professor Gehrkens often impressed on our minds that when it is misspelled "a capella," with only one "p," it really means "a little mountain goat."

A cappella is a term adopted in the early Renaissance period to designate a particularly pure style of choral music that developed in the late 15th century and reached its culmination 100 years later when Palestrina wrote for the Sistine Chapel of the Vatican. At first, the church authorities banned the use of any instruments in church services so that the choirs sang unaccompanied. But by the 17th century, a cappella church music was taken over by the cantata in which accompanying instruments played independent parts.

Now, the expression "a cappella" has come to describe any vocal music, religious or secular, that is sung unaccompanied. Church choirs would be much improved if the music director would require his singers to sing much of the music a cappella. The choir members would cease to rely on the pitches of the organ and be forced to listen to one another, thus developing a better sense of the whole relationship of their part with the others. As they progress in skill, they will begin to hear their chords ring true. With this experience, they will sing accompanied music much more beautifully.

CHAPTER XVI

Orchestral History

An orchestra is a large group of instrumentalists performing with string, woodwind, brass, and percussion instruments.

The word "orchestra" originally referred to the semicircular area within the play space of a classical Greek theater where the chorus danced.   In European opera houses of the 17th century the corresponding space was convenient to place the musicians, and the original name of the space was transferred to the musicians who occupied it.   Today, the word refers to any instrumental group that includes string instruments. Without the string section, the ensemble is called a band.

All kinds of instrumental groups containing a string instrument section are in existence today: chamber orchestras with ten to thirty instruments;   theater orchestras with ten to fifty musicians, usually playing in a pit at musical shows;   dance orchestras (sometimes erroneously called a dance band even when they have violins and string basses); opera orchestras; and symphony orchestras, which usually use the largest numbers of players.

Modern symphony orchestras vary in size from about sixty players to nearly 100, the common disposition being:

Strings
12 to 16 first violins
12 to 16 second violins
8 to 12 violas
6 to 10 cellos
4 to 9 string basses

Woodwinds
2 to 4 flutes and piccolos
2 to 4 oboes and English Horns
2 to 4 clarinets
2 to 4 bassoons

Brass
2 to 8 French Horns
2 to 4 trumpets
2 to 3 trombones
1 to 2 tubas

Percussion
2 to 5 timpani (usually played by one person) cymbals, triangles, snare drums, bass drum, gongs, xylophone, etc. (usually played by 2 or 3 players)

Each of the violin, viola, cello, and string bass sections of the orchestra play in unison and are treated by the composer much like an a cappella choir. The larger number of strings is needed to balance the power of the smaller number of wind instruments. For this reason, the louder instruments are placed behind the strings.

The leader of each section is usually called the "principal." The leader of the first violin section is called the "concertmaster." It is the concertmaster who calls for quiet, directs the oboist to sound the "A," and supervises the tuning-up procedure in preparation for the conductor to appear at the beginning of the program.

Orchestra history goes back to the earliest cultures in which percussion instruments were used to accompany songs and dances. There were orchestras several thousand years ago at the courts of Egypt and India, and the Emperor of China was said to have had more than 500 musicians who played string, woodwind, and percussion instruments. In the Old Testament is a description of King Nebuchadnezzar's orchestra consisting of strings, brasses, and woodwinds, all prototypes of our modern instruments.

The early European orchestras of the 16th century did not have parts written out for specific instruments. Each player was allowed to perform any part which he felt best suited the range of his instrument. It was not until the beginning of the 17th century that part writing for specific instruments was instituted by composers such as Gabrieli and Monteverdi.

The violin family was not perfected until the 17th century, when the musicians usually played while standing, the composer either at the harpsichord or serving as concertmaster, and the director beating time by pounding a wooden pole on the floor. Early 19th century composers began to demand more tonal qualities and agility of the players. As the instrumentalists' abilities increased, the orchestras grew larger, more sophisticated, and professional.

The first permanent professional orchestra was the Royal Philharmonic founded in 1813 in London. The Paris Conservatory Orchestra followed in 1828 and, in 1842, the New York Philharmonic and the Vienna Philharmonic. The Boston Symphony Orchestra started in 1881. Today, almost every important city in the world maintains a symphony orchestra. In the United States there are almost 1500.

In orchestrating compositions, the composer has in mind the instruments to play the melody, the chordal content, and the rhythmic pattern. The myriad orchestral colors are so important that the composer must have a clear and definite knowledge of the unique sounds produced on each instrument and the variation of tone color in each instrument's various registers. The composer must keep in mind not only the characteristic sound of each instrument, its range, and technical difficulty but also the changes in tone quality when doubled by one or more of the instruments in the other family sections. This puts a special responsibility on the conductor to faithfully reproduce the original sound conceived in the mind of the composer. A symphonic director, then, must be an expert in understanding instrumental problems and tonal colors if he is to be a success.

The range most customarily used by composers for string orchestra sections are:

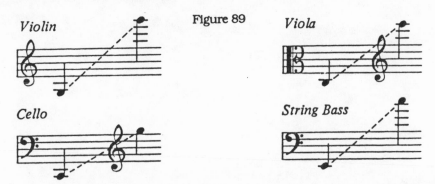

Figure 89

The string bass sounds an octave lower than written.

The strings, in flexibility and tone color, approach most closely the human voice but with a much greater range. Their expressive possibilities are almost infinite. To become a good orchestral musician demands more discipline than a football player, combines more social cooperation than required of a basketball player, requires more manual dexterity than a surgeon, and the accuracy of a fine mathematician. But whereas the mathematician may vaccillate between thinking and writing, the musician must make a quick, detailed decision and execute immediately with mathematical precision.

It is often true in our high schools that the best mathematicians are those who have tackled the difficulties of playing an instrument and have undergone the strict discipline of playing in an orchestra. Some of our greatest scientists are experts on some instrument, and in many cities businessmen and executives enjoy playing in symphony orchestras.

I have observed over the years that the best a cappella choirs and bands are in high schools and colleges that maintain a fine orchestra. There is a definite relationship to excellence. How tragic when a school superintendent emphasizes only band playing because of its value on a football field! Such a superintendent must be more interested in utilitarianism than in providing a good education.

CHAPTER XVII

Band History

A band is any group of wind instrument and percussion players that does not include instruments of the string family (with the possible exception of the string bass, which is often added to the symphonic band.)

There usually are three types of bands: the dance band, the military or marching band that performs at sports events and parades, and the concert band, which is often quite symphonic in sound and purpose.

The band appeared hundreds of years ago in Europe when groups of bugles and drums played tunes for foot soldiers to march to and to give battle signals. The band gradually expanded to include fifes, bagpipes, and drums. Oboes and clarinets later took the place of the bagpipes. It early became popular in Germany to maintain a town band that included trombone-type instruments and wooden cornets with finger holes. The latter were much like the instrument we know as the recorder.

By the 18th century, band concerts had become very popular in Europe, the ensemble consisting of oboes, bassoons, clarinets, and horns. As the century progressed, each European country took pride in its bands. The bands gradually grew in size until finally, in 1790, the French National Guard Band had reached seventy players.

By the late 18th century, European bands, influenced by the Turks, added bass drums, snare drums, cymbals, and triangles to their usual complement of kettledrums and military drums. The brilliant costumes of the Turks also inspired fancy uniforms and hats as well as drum majors and baton twirlers.

Napoleon and the French Revolution motivated the seventy-piece French National Guard Band and French composers to use every known type of wind instrument. The Guard started the National Conservatory of Music in Paris, which has become one of the world's most outstanding music schools.

The United States had military bands during the Revolutionary War, the earliest band still in existence being the United States Marine Corps Band, which was organized in 1798. The oldest permanent town band is the Allentown Band at Allentown, Pennsylvania, which was founded in 1828.

It was an Irish cornettist, Patrick Gilmore, who came to Massachusetts in the 1850s, who founded the first big concert band during the Civil War. After the war, he traversed the country organizing monstrous band festivals. To his own band of nearly eighty players, he would add other bands until the players would often number between 500 and 1000 musicians.

Gilmore's influence had a great effect on John Philip Sousa, the March King, who led the Marine Corps Band from 1880 to 1892. Sousa then left his post to form his own concert band group, which traveled all over the United States. Sousa's band made several tours of Europe and once went on an extensive concert tour around the world.

By this century, bands had become so sophisticated that major composers started to write a symphonic type of composition for concert bands. As early as 1911, the Goldman Band pioneered in commissioning composers to write band music. Men like Professor Arthur Williams of Oberlin College, once very active in the Music Educator's National Conference (MENC) and the National Band Master's Association, and prolific editor and author for band and music magazines, have been instrumental in bringing band performance up to the standard of our finest symphony orchestras.

The grouping of instruments on the pages of orchestra scores is now almost universal, whereas band scores because of different instrumentation from country to country have not yet been standardized. The United States has published the greatest treasure of band literature, both in original composition and in transcription arrangements, so I will display the normal American arrangement of instruments in a band score. The number of instruments on a part are not yet standard, but basically it is arranged by sections of sound quality. For this reason, you should direct a band more as you would a chorus with multiple voices. With an orchestra, which has fewer numbers and types of woodwinds and brass instruments, sections of sound give way to individual solo prominence.

Woodwind Choirs

Group I	Group II	Group III
Piccolo (D or C)	E Soprano Clarinet	E Alto Saxophone I and II
Flute I and II	B Clarinet I, II, III	B Tenor Saxophone
Oboe I and II	E Alto Clarinet	E Baritone Saxophone
English Horn	B Bass Clarinet	
Bassoon I and II		

Brass Choirs

Group I	Group II
B Cornet I, II and III	Trombone I, II and III
B Trumpet I and II	Baritone Horn I and II
French Horn I, II, III and IV	Tuba (plus String Bass)

Percussion

Of the various band instruments, the following sound as they are written on the staff or an octave higher or lower than written: piccolo in C, flute, oboe, heckel-phone in C, bassoon, contra bassoon, sarrusophone, B trombone, bass trombone, baritone horn (euphonium), tuba in E , tuba in C, and sousa-phone or tuba in B . Of the percussion instruments sounding musical pitches, the following sound as written or one or two octaves higher: celesta, tympani, xylophone, glockenspiel, vibraphone, and chimes.

Of all the instruments, the score generally indicates the pitch relationship. For example, see the following:

Transposing Instruments
Sounds *differing* fromwritten
(P = Perfect,   M = Major,   m = minor)

E Instruments	
Soprano Clarinet	m 3rd higher
Alto Clarinet	M 6th lower
Contra Bass Clarinet	8va + M 6th lower
Alto Saxophone	M 6th lower
Baritone Saxophone	8va + M 6th lower
D Instruments	
Soprano Clarinet	M 2nd higher
D Instruments	
Piccolo	8va—m 2nd higher
B Instruments	
Soprano Clarinet	M 2nd lower
Bass Clarinet (Treble Clef)	8va + M 2nd lower
Bass Clarinet (Bass Clef)	M 2nd lower
Contra Bass Clarinet	2—8va + M 2nd lower
Soprano Saxophone	M 2nd higher
Tenor Saxophone	8va + M 2nd lower
Bass Saxophone	2—8va +M 2nd lower
Cornet or Trumpet	M 2nd lower
Tenor Wagner Tuba	M 2nd lower

    A *Instruments*
        Soprano Clarinet   m 3rd lower
        Oboe D'Amore   m 3rd lower
    G *Instruments*
        Alto Flute   P 4th lower
    F *Instruments*
        English Horn   P 5th lower
        Basset Horn   P 5th lower
        French Horn   P 5th lower
        Bass Wagner Tuba   P 5th lower

The foregoing will probably help you to see why many conductors advocate that full band scores be written with all parts in the concert key, which would be written as it sounds, untransposed, even though the individual parts for the players would still retain the transposition. Fortunately, many publishers print a condensed score that is much abbreviated but sometimes not detailed enough. However, for a director, the orchestra score with an average of sixteen lines of parts is much easier to handle than the ordinary band score, which has anywhere from twenty-two to thirty-two lines.

CHAPTER XVIII

Score Reading

A score is the arrangement for all the parts, one above the other, that are to be sung or played together in a musical performance. The individual part for each voice or instrument is shown on a staff of its own (or sometimes sharing a staff with a similar instrument). The notes are vertically spaced so that all the notes indicating sounds meant to be heard simultaneously are lined up, one directly above the other. A vertical line would pass through all of them.

In an orchestra score, the woodwinds are generally placed at the top, followed by the brass instruments, then the percussion along with various specialized instruments such as the harp. Next are the soloists (for instance, in a concerto), followed by vocal parts (in a cantata or oratorio), all followed by the strings, which are located at the bottom of the score.

Within each group, the high-pitched instruments are placed near the top of the section, the lowest-pitched at the bottom. To help organize the page so that the eye can take it in at a glance, bar lines are drawn from top to bottom of each section but interrupted between sections all the way through the composition with the exception of the extreme left ahead of the signatures. In addition, parts for similar instruments are usually connected at the left hand beginning of each line by either a brace { or a heavy double line [, or sometimes both.

The word "score" comes from a name meaning the process of drawing lines through the music—that is, "scoring" or "marking off." Originally, music was most generally written in part books that contained only the part for a single performer. About 1600 some vocal and keyboard music began to appear in score form.

Even today, there are many examples of a "condensed score" or "short score." These are usually found with vocal scores in opera, oratorio, or cantata productions, or for instrumental soloists, in which the complicated full score is reduced to a piano type of accompaniment.

Figure 90 is a typical orchestral score. Notice the bar line and brace treatment to the left of the signatures and the differing key signatures for the transposing instruments: clarinet, French horn, and trumpet.

Figure 90

It is interesting that orchestra scores group the French horns with the woodwinds because the woodwind section quite often needs the horns for support. Band scores, on the other hand, because of the multiple number of woodwinds, including the saxophones, do not need to provide this kind of support. In band scores, the French horns, usually appear after the trumpets.

Also, in the orchestra score, the bassoon is at the bottom of the woodwind section, whereas in the band score it is grouped with the oboes to form a double-reed section. The band score differs by being arranged in choirs of sound and not so much by function.

As you will see in the following examples, a full score has certain advantages. The greatest is that it gives the conductor a complete display of all the parts played by each individual instrument, as well as the solo and chorus parts involved in the composition. You are not required to guess. Even the amateur director who does not have a thorough knowledge of orchestration or composition should have little difficulty if he has adequately studied the score ahead of time. All the detail is there before his eyes. The composer's voice-leading for each part is clearly evident.

Following are several examples:

Example I (figure 91) is a full orchestral score. Notice the bar lines separating each section, the lineup of the notes to be sounded simultaneously, the melody progression jumping from part to part, and the differing key signatures for the transposing instruments.

Example II (figure 92) is a page showing a score treatment involving a separation of the page into two sections of reduced score. This reduces the total number of pages required when there is an extended passage in which a number of instruments are silent or "tacet" and, therefore, need not be indicated.

Example III (figure 93) is an abbreviated or "condensed" band score.

As you may have already determined, there are some disadvantages to using a full score. The main one is that so many lines of staves cannot be comprehended by a quick glance of the eye. At most, the eye can focus on only one or two lines at a time. This makes it very probable that certain countermelodies and cues will be missed. This is remedied by many directors by marking the score with arrows or other symbols to attract the eye to all-important items.

You will notice that I said "all-*important* items." The marking should serve only to attract the eye. It is easy to overdo the markings. Too many symbols can be more distracting and confusing than the detail of the score itself. If you have become thoroughly acquainted with the elements of the score, a bare minimum of markings should be sufficient. A conductor must depend upon his mind as well as his eye. The eye functions by focusing on a particular detail with only limited recognition of the surrounding area. The director, therefore, must have a specific point of reference in each measure of the score and must have developed a mental association with that point of reference to know exactly what the other parts are doing.

Let's assume the melody in a particular passage is in the first violin. You naturally will choose the violin as your guideline for that passage. Having studied the score, your mind has associated an important countermelody with the oboe, the dynamic requirements of the brass instruments, the rhythmic pattern of the tympani, and any other important elements simultaneously present. The focal point of the eye is all-important only when it is coupled with detailed preparation that has established the necessary mental associations.

There is yet another problem when using a full score, primarily because the number of parts requires a full page to display all the staves. Eight measures per page is the normal average. When the left hand must turn the page, it cannot simultaneously be used in its normal function for dynamic control and cueing. It is often necessary for you to memorize a few measures on the next page in order to use the left hand effectively if the timing of turning the page would interfere. Turn the page only when the left hand is free of other requirements.

Now you can understand why in many instances a director might prefer a condensed score, particularly for a band. The condensed score will have many more measures per page, which reduces the page-turning problem, and may give a quicker comprehension of the entire composition. It also simplifies the greater complexities encountered in the band score. The disadvantage is that you may have to do some guessing regarding the mix of tone colors and particular cues that may have been omitted because of the simplification.

Your problem in score reading may be aggravated when a separation caused by a reduced score on the next page occurs. The oboe or the trumpet part may jump to a new position relative to the strings so that you might temporarily lose your visual orientation. In your preparation, it is imperative to spot the divided pages containing the abbreviated scores and, if necessary, to mark the right-hand margin of the previous page.

Whether using a full or condensed score, it is absolutely imperative that you be thoroughly familiar with the score before the first rehearsal. You must have absorbed it into your mind to the fullest extent so that you may have the freedom to establish and maintain necessary eye contact with your performers. Your all-inclusive familiarity with every important element will give you the ability to quickly scan a measure or even a page without the fear of missing any important cues, tempo, or dynamic markings. You will now be free to use your facial expressions, eye contacts, and hand techniques to the best advantage.

You may be tempted to consider yourself a director of a choir, orchestra, or band. But, not so! Never forget, you are the conductor of *music*. It is your responsibility to be faithful to the composer's intent.

Figure 91 (Example 1)

Figure 92 (Example 2)

Figure 93 (Example 3)

CHAPTER XIX

The Mystique of Conducting

Understanding the Mystery

Music is the mysterious, ethereal substance that blows gently from the heart of heaven. It is conceived in the mind of the composer, written down in abstract notes on paper that are, at best, only symbols subject to interpretation. But the music does not actually exist until it is performed. And because it is abstract, it never sounds exactly the same when played by any two different groups or even when performed consecutively by the same performer. Music is always dynamic, active, forceful, and everchanging.

Music notation is inexact and approximate. It is mysterious because it is so ambiguous. Even tempo and dynamic markings are subject to individual interpretations. Although music must be produced to become intelligible, there is, nevertheless, no physical contact with the sound except through the ear. Good music in performance stirs the air, vibrates the ear drum, and stimulates the mind to speak to the soul of the listener as well as the performer.

Good performance depends upon the conductor's feeling and understanding. It then becomes your responsibility to inspire the best from your performers by critical preparation and the ability to project your intentions to the group by clear, concise, and understandable conducting technique. Your duty is to work toward a technically acceptable performance that must be made spiritually meaningful, for all music emanates from the spirit and talks to the soul.

You must seek to identify with the composer's point of view. You should study and analyze every composition until it is so familiar that you might feel in your mind that you actually composed the music yourself.

This requires hard preparatory work, studying the phrasing, countermelodies, tempos, dynamics, tonal qualities, and climaxes as well as possible trouble spots. Only in this way will you be prepared to acquire a satisfactory sense of the sound contained in the score. Only by hard work in advanced preparation will you be able to form an opinion about the musical and spiritual meaning of the composition so that you can be sure to be ready to be the type of interpreter whom the musicians can respect.

Preparation

There is no substitute for a hard and critical study of the score in preparation for directing a number of musicians, be they professional or amateur. It may be even more important to study hard and critically with an amateur group because professionals can often carry the conductor through a temporary lapse of memory whereas amateurs do not usually have the ability or training to do so.

You must see the composition as a whole. You must know the total expanse of the work. Most professional performers do not. They know and understand, at most, their own part. Amateurs are incapable of seeing the whole, and much of your rehearsal time may be taken up with teaching them their part as well as leading them to recognize how their part fits into the overall picture. All performers, professional or amateur, are looking for a sense of security. Only the authority you have gained through proper conducting technique and a thorough and fine musical sense can give them that.

You must prepare your music ahead of the rehearsals. You must know and be aware of all the details of the composition as a whole, having studied the climaxes, tempos, opportunities for rubato, and expressive phrasing, and you must know the style of the composer. All this thorough study should be done in private in advance preparation for the rehearsal to command respect. It is musical respect for your stature as a knowledgeable conductor that builds confidence. It is crucial—the musicians must trust you and your judgment. Only by a thorough preparation can you be sure you are right. When you arrive at this understanding, then you are ready to kindly and lovingly lead your musicians, employing diplomacy, tact, and organizational skills with assurance and authority.

By studying the score thoroughly, you will develop a kind of sixth sense for handling any mishap and will develop confidence to know you will do a good job.

In the end, you cannot fool musicians, even amateurs. This is why a good background in the theory and practical application of good conducting techniques is so very important.

Fear not. Should a well-prepared director ever temporarily lose his place, the group will likely carry him on. Even the amateurs, if well rehearsed, will likely be able to do this. How different from the experience of the violinist who breaks a string or a soloist who forgets the words!

Function and Duty

The conductor functions as both the interpreter and as the master technician. He must be able to project the innate qualities of his personality and establish his authority not only by personal magnetism but, more important, be able to justify that authority by careful study and preparation. But none of these entities can be completely successful unless you have the technical acumen to communicate clearly and concisely with your musicians by expert baton and hand control.

A meaningful mental process is required of you. In rehearsal, you must listen critically and immediately take note of any points of difficulty. Be prepared to determine methods of correction, looking first to yourself, for you may have given a false or unclear signal that caused the confusion. If so, readily admit you are the one to blame. If not, kindly and graciously correct the culprit. You must take some kind of proper remedial action if the problem is to be solved. If you are to blame, analyze what it was you did and seek to improve your faulty technique.

At the performance, on the other hand, think ahead so as to prepare your musicians for the passages to come. Take the lead. Concentrate on the structure and balance of the composition as a whole in order to inspire the proper spirit and feeling in the performers because it is too late for any major corrections to be made. With amateur groups, anything can happen and usually does. But often, if you have the well-grounded technical ability to give clear signals, a sudden crisis can be avoided.

At rehearsals, do not waste time. Never use five words if two will do. Always be technically explicit. Always be friendly, even informal if the occasion permits, but always be precise and to the point. Be courteous; give the performer ample time to breathe both mentally as well as physically.

You should not let your ego dictate that musicians must do what *you* want. Always prepare thoroughly so that you will require your performers to do what the composer intends to be done. A good director is only an interpreter, a recreator who serves the composer faithfully. You must be equipped by temperament and technical ability to inspire the minds and spirits of your singers and instrumentalists to do their best to perform the composer's music in the way the composer conceived it. If you succeed, it will be very exciting for you as well as for the performers but more especially for the audience.

The podium should never serve as a monument to the conductor. The performers and the director are really music-making partners, all equal, only the responsibilities are different. If you treat your performers as subordinates, they will not give you their best efforts.

It is equally true that you should not consider yourself a star and conduct for the audience. A fine director conducts only for the music, to portray faithfully the ethereal inspiration in the mind of the composer that has blown so gently from the heart of heaven.

Technique

Certain of our great conductors have poor baton technique, often using a beat that is not always clear. They may employ strong gymnastic maneuvers inherent to their style but that certainly should not be copied as an ideal technique. They somehow produce good results because of their extraordinary personal magnetism and remarkable power to transmit energy through their eyes and body movements.

Baton and left-hand technique must be clear, precise, and concise to get super-excellent results. Every gesture should have a point, a musical reason to be, which makes it very easy to follow and understand. Superfluous, unessential gestures are both frustrating and distracting to the performers. If you have the ability to make clear your every intent, the players and singers will have confidence, will relax, and do their best.

Many conductors, understand the art of audience appeal and are able to manipulate the audience by showmanship. The truly great conductors, however, the ones who get the best from the performers, are those who possess a formidable and consistently effective baton technique. The baton is the focus of the entire conductor contact. If it is held too firmly with a stiff wrist and the elbow being the only moveable joint, it is inexpressive, the whole movement no better than an inflexible rod.

A good conductor does not need to hunch his shoulder at the neck. He will use all the other joints of the arm, the shoulder joint, elbow, wrist, and fingers in a flexible manner. If you use the baton, remember that your wrist must not flop downward from the straight line of the arm, and the baton should not be held sideward but be a straight-on extension of the arm.

The left hand, then, should be used only for any expression that is beyond the vocabulary of the baton technique. The left hand must *not* become *simply* the duplication of the movement of the baton, the only exception being the few instances when a cue might require a simultaneous movement. Here, of course, the right and left hands are serving separate functions even though they are moving in synchrony.

To direct without a baton in a large group sacrifices perceptive accuracy. A hand does not as easily define a point in space and, therefore, demands more critical observation on the part of the performers before the desired result can be obtained. It is usually effective to direct without a baton only with a small intimate ensemble. A large group such as a symphony, band, or comunity chorus can best react to the specific directions at the point of a baton.

A group of musicians will always reflect you as a result of your gestures. It is your control of the hardness or softness of the movement of arm, elbow, or wrist that can produce the necessary power, intensity, and decisiveness of response—but only if your gestures are efficient and clear.

It is not enough to direct in such a way as to be *understood.* Rather, your conducting should always be so clear as never to be *misunderstood.* Conducting technique should always be precise, sometimes relaxed, often intense, but always esthetic.

It is often difficult to accomplish all these concepts when amateurs have little or no previous musical training or ability, however much they enjoy the effort. As director of a German Club Chorus for a few years, these wonderful, sincere singers (always trying to teach me proper German pronunciation, which was confusing when they could not agree on it among themselves) told me that "Dirigent" was the German word for "Director." Whereupon, after a particularly frustrating night of rehearsal, I wrote the following poem:

The Baton Wielder

The trials and vicisitudes of a "Dirigent"
Are often beyond imagination
Tho' he try his best to be diligent,
The results are frequent disintegration.

He comes in a suit neatly pressed,
Wearing his best, most beautiful tie.
With explanations he hopes they're impressed,
But they blissfully shoot duck's with mind's eye.

He seeks to correct by example
A vowel that was produced too "white."
They think to a dark room they must trample
To find that "dark" vowel lost in light.

He selects varying songs in many tempos,
Songs not too difficult to do.

He corrects all their "Ahs" and their "Ohs"
But the result is a uniform "oo-oo."

He explains sound's path through the head,
How they should tickle their noses when they "hum,"
But later, after all has been said,
The Chorus thinks, "Dirigent is just dumb."

In his efforts he burns candles at both ends.
Small wonder hair drops from his scalp.
It's no effort at all—it distends
And falls out on its own without help.

Communication

It is a fact that the moment a new conductor steps on a podium for his first rehearsal with a new group, professional or amateur, the performers instantly sense whether or not he is a born conductor. After a few bars, you will be sized up both as a musician and as a person. Your preparation and authoritative control of conducting technique will always be manifest.

You must have a desire for leadership and enough ego and assuredness to inspire the group's confidence in you while maintaining enough modesty to assure their willing cooperation. If you love the music and can become completely absorbed in it, you will lose your ego in the interpretation. It is your duty to inspire everyone in your group to a oneness with the music.

You must be able to transmit your mental imagery to the musicians by your technical expertise. You cannot cheat or fool the performers. They will easily recognize if you are adequately prepared and whether you have well-grounded technique.

You must be able to communicate perfectly with your performers, the singers, and the instrumentalists who are the real stars of any performance. You must never allow yourself to put on a Ballet in which you become the star performer.

At rehearsals, you will explain what kind of sound you want by both succinct verbal instructions and expert baton and left-hand technique. But no matter how you approach the problems, this ensemble can never sound the same as another because your temperament, personality, and technique, coupled with the musicians' individual abilities, are never the same, even from day to day with the same group.

If you are to gain the greatest response from your musicians, do not stifle them. Overcontrol leads to insecurity. There is a fine line between being too lenient and being restrictive. You must travel the middle road. Ask for all the performers are capable of giving, but be satisfied with their best—particularly when dealing with amateurs.

At rehearsals, it is not always necessary to stop the group to correct a minor error. It may have been simply an accidental occurrence, never to recur. But if it happens again, then is the time to catch the culprit.

You will need a refined technical expertise to inspire your musicians to respond to every necessity of expression, phrasing, and dynamics. More important than anything else, however, is a great and deep love for the music and an abiding love for your musicians.

In amateur organizations, you must expect a performance full of technical flaws, but if everyone performs with enthusiasm as a response to your expertise and if the performance is built upon a love of music and each other, a satisfactory result will be obtained. You will have produced that mysterious "plus factor" that an audience can feel.

Approach all rehearsals and performances with good humor, warmth, charm, and conducting proficiency. Always let the performers, more particularly if they are amateurs, know when you are pleased. Creating a pleasant atmosphere will make the performers anxious to reciprocate.

If your efforts are sometimes greeted with indifference, do not become depressed. Remember that the sun often rises brilliantly in the East in the morning, but most of the audience continues to sleep on.

INDEX